THE BOUNDLESS CLASSROOM

Designing Purposeful Instruction for Any Learning Environment

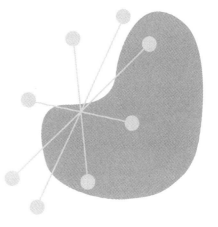

Nathan Lang-Raad and James Vince Witty

International Society for Technology in Education
PORTLAND, OREGON ▪ ARLINGTON, VIRGINIA

The Boundless Classroom:
Designing Purposeful Instruction for Any Learning Environment
Nathan Lang-Raad, Ed.D., and James Vince Witty, Ed.D., Esq.

Senior Director of Books and Journals: *Colin Murcray*
Senior Acquisitions Editor: *Valerie Witte*
Copyeditor: *Linda Laflamme*
Proofreader: *Lisa Hein*
Indexer: *Valerie Haynes Perry*
Book Design and Production: *Kim McGovern*
Cover Design: *Christina DeYoung*

Library of Congress Cataloging-in-Publication Data

Names: Lang, Nathan D., author. | Witty, James Vince, author.
Title: The boundless classroom : designing purposeful instruction for any learning
   environment / Nathan D. Lang-Raad, Ed.D., and James V. Witty, Ed.D., Esq.
Identifiers: LCCN 2021048934 (print) | LCCN 2021048935 (ebook) | ISBN 9781564849311
(Paperback) | ISBN 9781564849366 (ePub) | ISBN 9781564846907 (PDF)
Subjects: LCSH: Blended learning. | Teaching—Computer network resources. |
   Distance education—Computer network resources. | Internet in education. |
   Web-based instruction.
Classification: LCC LB1028.5.L7357 2022 (print) | LCC LB1028.5 (ebook) |
   DDC 371.3—dc23/eng/20211106
LC record available at https://lccn.loc.gov/2021048934
LC ebook record available at https://lccn.loc.gov/2021048935

First Edition
ISBN: 978-1-56484-931-1
Ebook version available

Printed in the United States of America

ISTE® is a registered trademark of the International Society for Technology in Education.

About ISTE

The International Society for Technology in Education (ISTE) is home to a passionate community of global educators who believe in the power of technology to transform teaching and learning, accelerate innovation and solve tough problems in education.

ISTE inspires the creation of solutions and connections that improve opportunities for all learners by delivering: practical guidance, evidence-based professional learning, virtual networks, thought-provoking events and the ISTE Standards. ISTE is also the leading publisher of books focused on technology in education. For more information or to become an ISTE member, visit iste.org. Subscribe to ISTE's YouTube channel and connect with ISTE on Twitter, Facebook and LinkedIn.

Related ISTE Titles

The Perfect Blend: A Practical Guide to Designing Student-Centered Learning Experiences, by Michele Eaton
iste.org/PerfectBlend

Distance Learning for Elementary STEM: Creative Projects for Teachers and Families, by Amanda Thomas
iste.org/ElementarySTEM

About the Authors

Nathan Lang-Raad, Ed.D., is an international speaker, author, and professional learning facilitator. He is Vice President of Strategy at Savvas Learning (formerly Pearson). Prior to joining Savvas, he was Chief Education Officer at WeVideo. He has served as a teacher, principal, university adjunct professor, consultant, and education strategist throughout his career. He was the director of elementary curriculum and instruction for Metropolitan Nashville Public Schools and the education supervisor at NASA's Johnson Space Center. He is the co-founder of Bammy Award–nominated #LeadUpChat, an educational leadership professional learning network (PLN) on Twitter. Previously, he was the president-elect of the ISTE Education Leaders Professional Learning Network. Lang-Raad is the author of *Everyday Instructional Coaching*; co-author of *The New Art and Science of Teaching Mathematics* with Dr. Robert J. Marzano; author of *WeVideo Every Day*; co-author of *Mathematics Unit Planning in a PLC at Work, Grades PreK–2*; and co-author of *The Teachers of Oz: Leading with Wisdom, Heart, Courage, and Spirit* with Herbie Raad. He resides in the beautiful state of Maine with his husband, Herbie. To learn more about Lang-Raad's work, visit drlangraad.com or follow him on Twitter and Instagram @drlangraad.

James Vince Witty, Ed.D., Esq. is a Tennessee native with 20 years of experience working for and on behalf of students and families. Dr. Witty currently serves as Executive Director of Schools within the Metropolitan Nashville Public Schools district, leading and supporting high schools. He earned a Bachelor's degree and a Master's degree from Middle Tennessee State University. Witty also received a Doctor of Education degree from the University of Tennessee and, most recently, a Doctor of Jurisprudence degree from the Nashville School of Law. At the national level, Witty is known for authoring *Exemplary Practices in Alternative Education: Indicators of Quality Programming*, published by the National Alternative Education Association. He has served students, teachers, and families as a teacher, an executive principal, an adjunct professor, a district leader, and a director for the Tennessee Department of Education. Witty is also the founding executive principal of MNPS Virtual School, Tennessee's first public virtual school. In 2019, Witty was recognized as Principal of the Year for his school district. More recently, in his role as Executive Director of Schools, Witty is responsible for sustaining learning continuity during the COVID-19 pandemic by scaling remote, virtual, and blended learning options for students.

Acknowledgments

Nathan's Acknowledgments

I always enjoy writing this part, because I get to reflect and show gratitude for the people who have supported and encouraged me.

First to my family:

To my husband, Herbie, for always and unconditionally supporting my ability to take on more than I should at any given time. I couldn't do any of this without your love, encouragement, inspiration, warmth, wit, and support.

To my son, Clayton, and my daughter, Anna, your courage, independence, and strength daily push me to be the best father I can be.

To my mom, Sheila, your kind, nurturing, and caring spirit is beyond beautiful.

I want to thank my co-author and co-collaborator, James. It's been amazing to bring all of our work together, to tap into your creativity and brain, and to learn from you along the way. I also want to thank my good friend and daily thought partner, David Moore; your friendship and support help me think deeper about life and work. Thank you to Valerie, our lead editor at ISTE, for your hard work, guidance, and feedback.

James' Acknowledgments

At this crossroads, it is with great respect and gratitude that I honor those individuals who have supported me in writing this book, my first book, *The Boundless Classroom*. First and foremost, to my co-author, Nathan. Thank you for inspiring me to achieve greatness and supporting me in this endeavor. To Valerie, our lead editor and friend. Your knowledge, expertise, and support brought this dream to life. To my mom, Tracy Singel, my success as an individual is a testament to your success as a mother. All that I am and hope to be, I owe to you. Finally, to my husband, Jesse Heath Walker, I thank you for your love, inspiration, support, and encouragement. Together, there isn't anything we cannot achieve or overcome. I love you the "mostest."

Publisher's Acknowledgments

ISTE gratefully acknowledges the contributions of the following:

ISTE Standards Reviewers

Meredith Boullion

Billy Krakower

Karen Lipski

Daniel Thomas

Vanessa Waxman

Manuscript reviewers

Nancy Baltodano

Eileen Belastock

Rich Dixon

Contents

Introduction..x

CHAPTER 1
Learning Lessons from the Pandemic and Implications for the Future.......................1

    Outcomes for Professional Learning..1

    Clarity and Simplicity..2

    Asynchronous and Synchronous Learning...3

    Professional Development...4

    Consistency...4

    Feedback..4

    Everyone's Well-Being...5

    Challenges and Strategies for Teaching in a Concurrent Classroom.........................5

    Collaboration..6

    Student Products...6

    Think-Alouds and Read-Alouds...7

    Social-Emotional Learning...8

    Assessment..9

    Learning Interruption, Not Learning Loss..9

    Personalized Learning...11

    Conclusion..15

CHAPTER 2
Planning Essentials for Blended Learning and Beyond..17

    Outcomes for Professional Learning..17

    Exploring Blended Learning Models..19

    Planning and Implementation Actions for Blended Learning Success......................22

    Conclusion..43

CHAPTER 3
Mapping the Course Scope and Sequence...45

    Outcomes for Professional Learning..45

    Formulating Course Objectives..47

    Creating Outcomes for Student Learning...49

Contents

Organizing and Sequencing Units and Lessons 56

Aligning Assessments.. 59

Conclusion.. 62

CHAPTER 4

Constructing a Pacing Guide and Establishing Learning Expectations............................ 65

Outcomes for Professional Learning 65

Examining Pacing Guide Essentials 69

Designing a Pacing Guide Checklist.. 86

Evaluating a Pacing Guide Template 88

Conclusion.. 90

CHAPTER 5

Designing and Delivering Blended Instruction.. 91

Outcomes for Professional Learning 91

Design Essential #1: Open with Optimism 93

Design Essential #2: Communicate Learning Outcomes..................................... 97

Design Essential #3: Activate Prior Knowledge 99

Design Essential #4: Build Academic Vocabulary 100

Design Essential #5: Deliver Engaging Instruction 106

Design Essential #6: Facilitate Student Discourse.. 111

Design Essential #7: Close with Optimism 115

Design Essential #8: Extending Learning Through Feedback and Reflection 120

Conclusion 121

CHAPTER 6

Designing and Delivering Virtual Instruction 123

Outcomes for Professional Learning 123

Design Essential #1: Introduce the Lesson and Communicate the Learning Outcomes 125

Design Essential #2: Activate Prior Knowledge 129

Design Essential #3: Build Academic Vocabulary 131

Design Essential #4: Deliver Engaging Instruction.. 134

Design Essential #5: Provide Opportunities to
Self-Assess and Automated Feedback for Students... 143

Design Essential #6: Create Closure and Preview the Assessment...................... 147

Conclusion 151

CHAPTER 7

Engaging Students with Authentic Assessments 153

    Outcomes for Professional Learning 153

    Measuring Learning with Assessments 156

    Engaging Students with Portfolios, Performance Tasks, and Products 157

    Effective Formative Assessments.. 159

    Designing Engaging and Authentic Assessments 163

    Creating an Assessment Plan.. 168

    Conclusion.. 176

CHAPTER 8

Maximizing Academic Feedback.. 179

    Outcomes for Professional Learning 179

    Defining Feedback.. 181

    Quality Feedback Essentials 182

    Feedback Norms.. 185

    Feedback as a Formative Assessment Strategy.. 187

    Differentiating Feedback 188

    Feedback Protocols 190

    Conclusion.. 199

CHAPTER 9

Integrating Digital Citizenship 201

    Outcomes for Professional Learning 201

    Strategies and Skills for the Digital Age 203

    Building Context for Digital Citizenship.. 204

    Framing Digital Citizenship 205

    Integrating Digital Citizenship into the Classroom.. 207

    Conclusion.. 209

Epilogue 211

    Commitment 1: Commit to Yourself 211

    Commitment 2: Commit to Your Colleagues.. 212

    Commitment 3: Commit to Your Students 213

References 215

Index 219

Introduction

When the COVID-19 pandemic struck in early 2020, it created the largest disruption of education systems in history, affecting over a billion learners globally. Closures of schools and other learning spaces impacted most of the world's students. During this time, teachers challenged old ways of thinking and experimented with professional strategies and practices. Students experienced innovation and personalization like never before, and they will continue demanding that our profession progress.

The pandemic also magnified pre-existing education disparities by reducing learning opportunities for many of our most vulnerable students, including those living in poor or rural areas, and students with disabilities. School leaders had to grapple with how to establish continuity of learning to close out the year in which the pandemic began and begin the next school term (even when leaders weren't sure this would happen).

During this time, many districts turned to a remote or distance learning model, with students learning from home using a school-provided or student-provided device. Eventually, many districts employed phased reopening plans, depending on the percentage of active COVID-19 cases. Some schools went back to in-person instruction, but many used either a hybrid model or continued remote/distance learning. Under the hybrid model, students typically attended in-person school two days a week and distance learning three days a week (or some similar combination of in-person and remote instruction). This proved difficult for most districts, as they faced many struggles: inequities for devices and internet connectivity for students, absenteeism (not showing up for synchronous, remote class meetings), and teachers' need for support in distance learning strategies.

Teachers and school leaders had to focus on those standards that were the most critical for student success in the next grade. Some states and districts provided guidance for these prerequisites in reading/ELA, math, science, and social studies for each grade level/course. In addition, educators focused on maximizing student engagement during remote learning through:

- Real-world connections to learning (finding curriculum connections or teacher-identified connections)

- Gamified, self-paced learning platforms that provided frequent and automated feedback

- Consistent, actionable feedback on student work/learning, with celebrations of progress

- Project-based learning on engaging, socially relevant topics, with clear links to standards, learning supports for students, as well as extension or enrichment opportunities

Today, districts and schools continue to enhance and refine their remote learning plans. As they move forward and prepare for the future, district and school leaders are actively reinforcing the following principles:

- Enriching connections between educators and students as well as social-emotional learning (SEL)

- Accessing academic content 247 with an emphasis on applying and deepening previously taught knowledge and skills

- Specifying times each day for exercise, practice, intervention, and enrichment activities

- Prioritizing meaningful connections between students and their peers

- Engaging core instruction focused on the prerequisite content standards that are most critical for student success in the next grade level

- Increasing experiential learning opportunities (students learning from the world around them)

- Personalizing learning based upon the distinct needs, interests, aspirations, or cultural backgrounds of students

- Streamlining and enhancing communications with students and their families to optimize accessibility to teachers and other school leaders

The Boundless Classroom covers all this and more, offering many opportunities to move forward, with clear frameworks and aligned practices to remove barriers typically associated with blended learning. It is designed to help you meet the needs of all your learners: those watching an instructional video from home, giving and receiving feedback remotely, and working in a brick-and-mortar classroom. We've included specific, easy-to-implement strategies that leverage lessons learned from synchronous and asynchronous learning as well as in-person and remote learning experiences. Whether you're teaching full time in person, implementing hybrid learning, or teaching full time remotely, you will find useful strategies that are specifically aligned to the mode of teaching and learning that you're currently implementing.

With all the changes that continue to unfold, only one thing is for certain: There is no such thing as a "return to normal." Most educators agree that "normal" didn't work, even prior to the pandemic. We were operating in an antiquated system. So, why should we return to that reality? Educators are now faced with a unique opportunity to approach teaching and learning in new ways, based on the challenges, solutions, and innovations experienced during the pandemic.

Any sustainable change must be aligned to a collaboratively developed vision within a purposeful community. Visioning comes from a clear sense of the problem at hand and an open-minded approach to solving it. When given a well-defined structure and order to operate inside of, we're empowered to create and problem-solve to achieve our goals and the goals of our purposeful community. We have the ability to create the change we've always wanted to see in education. Now, more than ever, is the time for lasting, meaningful change to many of our antiquated teaching and learning practices.

Through purposeful integration of instructional technologies, you can create meaningful and challenging learning opportunities for all your students, no matter the modality in which you teach. We invite you to explore the strategies and approaches we have shared in the pages that follow, to deepen your practice, and to reimagine the learning you can bring into your classroom.

CONNECTING TO THE ISTE STANDARDS

 The ISTE Standards are your road map to helping students become empowered learners. These standards deepen your practice, promote collaboration with peers, challenge you to rethink traditional approaches, and prepare students to drive their own learning. To help you connect the professional learning in this book to the ISTE Standards for Educators, we've included the relevant indicators at the beginning of each chapter. Scan the QR code or visit iste.org/standards/for-educators to view the ISTE Standards for Educators in full.

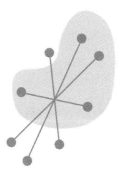

CHAPTER 1

Learning Lessons from the Pandemic and Implications for the Future

Outcomes for Professional Learning

In this chapter, we'll discuss:

- Teaching during the COVID-19 outbreak

- Learning and instructional strategies that were effective during the pandemic

- Identifying and maximizing effective remote learning practices to scale

- Planning for the post-COVID-19 classroom

CONNECTING TO THE ISTE STANDARDS FOR EDUCATORS

The content of this chapter relates to the following indicators:

Learner (2.1.c) Educators stay current with research that supports improved student learning outcomes, including findings from the learning sciences.

Facilitator (2.6.a) Educators foster a culture where students take ownership of their learning goals and outcomes in both independent and group settings.

Analyst (2.7.a) Educators provide alternative ways for students to demonstrate competency and reflect on their learning using technology.

Analyst (2.7.c) Educators use assessment data to guide progress and communicate with students, parents and education stakeholders to build student self-direction.

It's clear that the time for considering major reform in education is now. After all, while the pandemic was temporary (although experts say we might be dealing with the effects for years to come), some things we've learned during this time might not be. Over the past year, we, Nathan and James, have reflected on the challenges and disruptions in America's schools and also witnessed pockets of success in spite of these challenges. Here are our biggest observations and reflections on the most pressing needs of students—and their teachers.

Clarity and Simplicity

Clarity and simplicity are key. During the pandemic, there was a lot of confusion about how students would engage in learning or how assessments would be executed (or whether they should be). With any change, even in a "normal" year, educators need very clear expectations—and those expectations must be communicated concisely and consistently. When schools began to require remote and distance learning, a lot of ambiguity surrounded strategies and best practices. It seemed as if everyone was producing remote learning resources from scratch. San Gabriel Unified is a small Title I district in Los Angeles. During the pandemic, leaders reflected on what was happening to their students, their families, their staff, and their community. Leaders purposefully took time to talk to all of their stakeholders: students, parents, teachers, local business owners, outside experts, and educators from other schools and districts in Los Angeles and beyond. Leaders asked what was working and what wasn't. Grounded with that information, the district quickly adapted their instructional approaches to meet the needs of all students. Leaders then quickly communicated changes to all stakeholders with clarity and simplicity.

Similar conversations are happening today regarding the future of teaching and learning. District and school leaders are now reflecting on the successes realized during the pandemic and questioning, "What do we want to see stick moving forward?" As future plans continue to formalize, educators need structure and a plan, and inside of that structure they needed digestible and implementable ideas that are clear and simple to implement.

Asynchronous and Synchronous Learning

A fundamental debate of remote learning revolves around one question: Which is more effective: synchronous ("live") learning with students connected to a teacher live using Google Hangouts or Zoom, or asynchronous learning that allows students to access content and learn at their own pace? The latter option allows time during the school day for educators to provide synchronous support to students in critical need of direct instruction. During the pandemic, accessibility for all students and conflicting family commitments or responsibilities during the school day also factored into the effectiveness equation. Ensuring that students could watch lessons multiple times, as needed, while completing assignments was a struggle, as well. As a result, many teachers were tasked with, for the first time, creating on-demand instructional videos and other digital resources to support student learning.

For many districts and schools, a combination of learning opportunities and strategies was the best solution. Teachers found that student-centered "opportunity learning" was motivating and connected students to their everyday world, whether it was cooking with family members or trying to reason through a math problem about the shadow cast of an outside tree. Teachers quickly adapted, creating instructional videos and other digital learning resources so that students could engage in mini-lessons, think-alouds, and modeling. Synchronous meetings also became an effective social-emotional learning (SEL) opportunity, ensuring that teachers could connect with their students in meaningful ways during a traumatic time.

Professional Development

Because teachers were instructing from home, the professional development model of gathering in the library at the end of the school day (which wasn't always effective anyway) needed to change. A new flexibility to engage in and access non-traditional professional development opportunities arose. Educators shared experiences, support, and ideas (often just in time) using tweets, social posts, blogs, vlogs, podcasts, vodcasts (video podcasts), webinars, and more. The pandemic afforded teachers new ways to access professional development and quickly adjust their practices to meet the challenging and changing learning conditions associated with the pandemic.

Consistency

Meanwhile, students struggled with attention residue. A term coined by University of Washington business professor Sophie Leroy, *attention residue* is the negative effect on the mind of a learner when asked to switch a task or upon experiencing an interruption. At any one time, for example, a student might be juggling thoughts such as, "The teacher wants me to use Google Classroom, and the teacher just emailed me a video. The teacher also mailed me a hard-copy packet—do I need to look at that first?—and a different teacher asked me to use Google Forms for assessments." The more things we ask students to open and the more times they must flip back and forth between tools (applications, platforms, and technologies), the more likely students will expend cognitive energy that's already being competed for in trying to learn from home—not to mention the many distractions that come from learning at home. During the pandemic, consistency was more important than ever: choosing a single tool or a few tools and sticking with them across the entire school or district. Consistency offers familiarity and consistency for students. With so many available tools, it's essential to find one that is easy, fun to use, and engages students.

Feedback

Feedback and assessment finally clicked with each other during the 2020–2021 school year. With the lack of in-person interactions, feedback became even more crucial than ever before. Many schools minimized the importance of letter grades (something education reformers have been pushing for years) and emphasized high-quality, actionable feedback for students. The challenge was how to give timely, specific, and measurable feedback in a consistent manner—a question we'll tackle in Chapter 8, "Maximizing Academic Feedback." Every student's creation or response deserves feedback and warm affirmation. It lets students know that we care about them and their learning, especially during challenging times.

Everyone's Well-Being

As teachers, we knew our students faced daily stress and trauma during the pandemic, so we did everything we could to ensure that they felt cared for and valued. We also learned that after eight hours of Zoom meetings, we needed to prioritize our own self-care. It's important that you take care of yourself and teach others how to do this. What does that mean exactly? Consider the following:

- Check in with how you are feeling a few times per day.

- Be kind to yourself and flexible (as permitted) with your schedule.

- Find a "tech" routine that works for you and your family.

- Accept that time is limited, everything can't be accomplished, and focus on the practices that have the greatest impact for students.

- Take meta-moments, giving yourself and everyone around you the permission to feel all emotions: happy, sad, angry, hopeful, calm, stressed, and more.

Challenges and Strategies for Teaching in a Concurrent Classroom

One of the biggest challenges resulting from the pandemic was the concurrent classroom, also called the *HyFlex classroom*. The name suggests a hybrid or high-flexibility approach, but ironically, it's not anywhere near as easy to implement as the name connotes. In this environment, teachers are charged with simultaneously instructing and engaging students in two uniquely different learning environments: in person in a brick-and-mortar classroom and remotely on a computer at home. Concurrent classrooms present challenges for the students, as well. Online students often feel disadvantaged and that they don't have equal access to the teacher. When teachers tailor and focus instruction for online learners, in-person students experience similar frustrations.

To ensure both in-person and online students receive equitable instruction, instructional videos are a viable solution. This enables all students to access and view instructional materials outside of the synchronous classroom setting. By creating instructional videos, teachers ensure equal opportunities for both in-person and online students to learn. This option offers equitable experiences for students, as all receive the same content in the same manner. By recording the direct asynchronous instruction portion for students to watch prior to the synchronous meeting (online or in person), teachers are also able to provide targeted, direct instruction to struggling learners. This, in turn, allows teachers to focus synchronous time (in person or online) on SEL connections, application of concepts, creativity opportunities, and small-group collaborations. (For tips on creating effective instructional videos, see Chapter 5, "Designing and Delivering Blended Instruction.")

Collaboration

Collaboration can and should occur in online and in-person environments. During the pandemic, teachers quickly found ways to integrate collaborative opportunities for students as a means to engage learners. Students working in person could concurrently collaborate with students at home using cloud-based applications, for example. The key to success is ensuring that collaborative environments are thoughtfully designed and include clear expectations and guidance from teachers. Students crave autonomy and agency, but autonomy and agency work only if you've provided clear instructions on the task, an interesting and relevant problem to solve, or question prompts that allow for multiple ideas and solutions.

Student Products

Sharing and presenting their work is challenging for students in a concurrent classroom; students at home have difficulty hearing what students are saying in the classroom and vice versa. Additionally, students engage more when they're able to see visual representations of their peers' ideas and responses. Video creations, presentations, and other digital visual representations are equally effective in a traditional in-person classroom as well as an online classroom. For example, you can post videos in Google Drive or Google Classroom and give students a timeframe of when videos must be viewed. For optimal success, provide rubrics for students to review peer videos and provide a clear structure for providing feedback to one another.

Think-Alouds and Read-Alouds

Think-alouds and read-alouds can still occur even if students don't show up for synchronous online instruction. Think-alouds and read-alouds can be quite engaging for asynchronous instruction, which provides more time for students to reflect on problems they're solving or the text they're reading. It also provides flexibility for students; they get to choose when they're ready to interact, and they can go back and listen to parts of the video as many times as they want. This was extremely important during the pandemic as many students were learning independently.

When thinking aloud, it's also helpful for students to see visual representations of what they are learning. To help facilitate this, create a screen recording. Model a math problem on a digital whiteboard, for example, or build a concept map around a new vocabulary word. When you're finished, most recording tools will automatically insert the screen recording into your instructional video. With this quick activity, you've addressed the unique needs of visual learners that prefer visual representations as opposed to simply listening.

Additionally, think-alouds offer embedded research-based instructional strategies such as KWLs (Know, Want to Know, Learned), higher-order questioning, close reading, the Frayer Model, reasoning through math problems, and more right into your instructional video. This allows all students to engage asynchronously no matter if concurrent, online, or in-person.

Read-alouds were also effective. Reading aloud helps students process information, increasing their vocabulary and comprehension. This strategy supports auditory students that learn best by listening. During the pandemic, teachers quickly adapted this traditional instructional strategy by recording read-alouds for students. When recording a read-aloud, make sure you pause often, thinking aloud or asking questions of students. While an asynchronous event, thinking aloud and asking questions will only further engage students in their learning. When you prompt their thinking with questioning, be sure to give students time to think about their answers. For example, insert thirty seconds of soft music in the recording or tell students to pause the video. (Chapter 5 offers more examples and prompts for instructional videos.)

Social-Emotional Learning

Social-emotional learning (SEL) has been recognized by many as the most important issue of the pandemic. The Collaborative for Academic, Social, and Emotional Learning (CASEL) defines SEL as "the process through which all young people and adults acquire and apply the knowledge, skills, and attitudes to develop healthy identities, manage emotions and achieve personal and collective goals, feel and show empathy for others, establish and maintain supportive relationships, and make responsible and caring decisions" (n.d.). It will be years before we fully understand the impact on social-emotional health and learning of students due to the pandemic. Many lost important time for connecting with peers and engaging in social learning experiences. Many students experienced acute isolation and are still battling disconnection, anxiety, stress, and depression. Through regular, online synchronous meetings and asynchronously, students did communicate with teachers about their feelings and progress in their learning. Despite all the talk about social-emotional health during the pandemic, many still question how to address the identified needs of students. As you move forward, the following questions will help you address SEL foci in your classroom:

- How do I focus on creating a safe, nurturing, and connected space and time for the important work of developing meaningful and lasting relationships?

- How will I collaboratively plan for integrating SEL into daily routines and lessons?

- How will I begin every day or every lesson in a way that invites and establishes inclusion, safety, interconnection, and belonging before introducing new learning?

- How will I end every day or every lesson with learners reflecting and looking forward on a positive note?

- How will I embed time to listen to students' fears and anxieties and support them by providing blended learning opportunities, access to counseling, and opportunities for individual expression, as well as by creating positive spaces to be open and transparent?

By creating space and an intentional focus to support the cognitive, social, emotional, and physical wellbeing of students, we prioritize the health of our communities and families over grades, assessments, accountability, and so on. As we know, learning is most challenging if we've not first addressed the basic needs of our students.

Assessment

The life skills required to navigate the pandemic couldn't be measured by traditional assessments. So many districts shifted away from giving grades and focused on providing authentic assessment (text-based or video), often using tools they already had in place. Stakeholders debated whether diagnostic assessments would be helpful in providing specific data on which students were being reached and which were not. Yet others questioned the quality of the data existing assessments yielded for diagnosing individual student needs. And some expressed concern about the potential interruption of instructional time and the misplaced focus on catching up students. Overall, giving timely and specific feedback was, and is, an effective form of formative assessment. We will talk more about formative and authentic assessments within a blended learning environment in Chapter 7, "Engaging Students with Authentic Assessments."

Learning Interruption, Not Learning Loss

The term learning loss entered the lexicon of education jargon as educators tried to articulate the major impact the pandemic had on student learning. Many students saw their teachers only through a computer screen, whereas some were able to access their teachers in person a couple of days a week or more. But students interacting in different ways doesn't equate to a year's loss of learning. The term framed the conversation negatively before educators could even grasp, assess, or understand where students were in their learning. Nor does it account for the major advancement of students' digital age learning skills during this time. In this book, we will use the term learning interruption, as proposed by a few, to create a more empowering frame for approaching this subject and to avoid making any assumptions about learning impact.

During the pandemic, the nation's 13,000 districts largely devised their own standards for when it was safe to reopen schools and what COVID-19 mitigation measures to use. While many students learning remotely clearly were falling behind, few districts comprehensively assessed where their students were or what skills they had and had not learned during the pandemic. Yet, learning disruption was (and remains) a major concern for school and district leaders. Schools had to make creative decisions about how students would access high-quality instruction, and educators had to quickly adapt, providing differentiated (flipped learning instructional videos) and personalized (multimodal formative assessment) instruction for all students.

Preliminary data and findings from those studies that were conducted indicate that the disruption of education has not affected everyone equally. For instance, districts serving high percentages of nonwhite or poor students were significantly more likely to remain fully remote during the fall of 2020 than other districts. Some other key findings from the NWEA, Renaissance, and McKinsey & Company (Dorn et al., 2020) studies identified during the 2020–2021 school year follow.

The NWEA study (Kuhfeld et al., 2020) found:

- In fall of 2020, students in grades 3 through 8 performed similarly in reading to same-grade students in the fall of 2019 and about five to ten percentile points lower in math.

- In certain grades, Hispanic and Black students experienced lower scores in reading.

The Renaissance study (Renaissance, 2021) determined:

- Reading scores on average were one percentage point below typical levels, while math scores fell about seven points.

- Students in grades 4 through 7 will need an average of four to seven weeks to catch up in reading, based on Renaissance's translation of learning disruption into terms of instructional time. Students in grades 5 and 6 were more than twelve weeks behind in math, and students in grades 2, 3, 4, 7, and 8 will need four to eleven weeks to meet the expectations for the beginning of a typical school year.

The McKinsey & Company study found:

- White students experienced one to three months of learning disruption in math.

- Students of color experienced three to five months learning disruption in math.

- Other variables identified include whether students returned to school in-person, received improved remote instruction, or continued with existing distance learning models of mixed quality.

Based on researcher findings, the McKinsey & Company study (Dorn et al., 2020) made the following recommendations:

- Emphasize equitable access to high-quality math teaching and learning.

- Engage in mixed-level groupings.

- Maintain high expectations for learning.

- Provide differentiated support for each student.

- Offer exposure to grade-level content, while scaffolding students with "just-in-time support" so they can access such content.

- Reimagine elements of curriculum, teaching, technology, and supporting infrastructure in ways that go beyond the norm.

- Ensure high-quality instructional materials.

- Integrate best practices in personalized, blended learning options.

- Build systematic opportunities for engagement, collaboration, and feedback.

Personalized Learning

Personalized learning refers to instruction in which the pace of learning and the instructional approach are optimized for the needs of each learner. As districts have worked through the challenges of various distance learning environments, this approach has attained a great focus. By their very nature, remote and blended classrooms provide more opportunities for personalized learning to be practiced.

Even before the pandemic, many educators agreed that personalized, student-centered learning was more effective overall than the traditional, teacher-centered model, which maintains a fixed curriculum and pace. By embracing a more personalized approach to teaching and learning, educators can provide a more effective path for students, offering them the space and time necessary to master learning objectives rather than restricting learning to a traditional classroom setting or format. We will apply a lens of personalized learning throughout the book in the tools and strategies we share with you.

STOP. REFLECT. PLAN. ACT.

Lessons Learned and Future Implications

Professional Learning Task. In this section, we discussed lessons learned during the pandemic as well as future implications. Take a moment to **stop**, **reflect**, **plan**, and **act**. After reflecting, use the space below to identify five lessons learned during the pandemic as well as implications relative to future instructional practice. Consider what new instructional practices you plan to retain, as well as any antiquated practices that you plan to abandon.

1.

2.

3.

4.

5.

Now that educators have cleared the hurdle of getting school up and running during a global pandemic, education leaders as well as policymakers must look for ways to seize upon this moment and fully scale student-centered and personalized practices in the post-COVID-19 classroom. For school systems where pockets of student-centered practices already flourish, administrators should support innovative teachers. One simple starting point: Increase educators' access to edtech tools that support student-centered practices and mastery-based progression, as well as professional development that makes adopting student-centered learning more manageable. Teachers who are early adopters of student-centered practices can train and coach willing colleagues.

School leaders who influence policy and funding play an important role in encouraging educators and other leaders to adopt student-centered and personalized practices. They can introduce goals and norms that align schools' priorities with student-centered practice, such as focusing on student well-being and social-emotional learning. In addition, school leaders must provide access to online learning systems that help schools track student learning growth on a regular basis.

FROM THE FIELD
Portland's Outdoor Classroom

Portland Public Schools (PPS), in Maine, includes seventeen schools that serve 6,750 students in grades PK–12. PPS was one of the first public school districts in the country to develop a district-wide outdoor learning program for the 2020–2021 school year in response to COVID-19.

This new program with district-wide leadership and school board support built on an existing network of smaller school garden and outdoor learning projects that individual teachers and schools created and led in previous years. The current district-wide program helped align these efforts and build on them with new investments distributed across all school campuses. This newly expanded effort addressed the pandemic, while also laying the foundation for a long-term outdoor learning program in the years to come.

PPS gave families a choice about how they wanted their students to return to school for the 2020–2021 school year. Roughly 1,000 students requested to have school completely online in a Remote Academy, so PPS created a new, separate district-wide remote learning program for them. The remaining students (approximately 5,000) chose a hybrid learning model that included in-person instruction two days a week at school and remote learning from home two days a week. No classes were held on Wednesdays, to give teachers enough time for preparation and student outreach.

PPS created a total of 156 outdoor classrooms across the district. Each of these outdoor classrooms is designed to seat ten to twelve students, so the overall outdoor classroom capacity across the district is approximately 1,800 students. Thirty-three of the outdoor classrooms across the district have shade sails, created by a local company. Most of the outdoor classrooms use large five-gallon buckets and stumps as individual seats for the students. The buckets also act as personal storage containers for each student, holding their supplies. PPS worked with local distilleries who donated hundreds of these bucket-seats. The district also purchased additional buckets, as well as camp chairs for teachers, to meet their seating needs.

PPS worked with the United Way of Greater Portland and the local carpenters' union 349 to build 204 outdoor easels to hold whiteboards for each of the outdoor classrooms. Rolling file carts were purchased for teachers to move supplies outside. The district also provided each of the 5,000 students with their own "learning kit," which included a drawstring backpack, a clipboard, notebooks, and pens. The personal learning kits helped the students avoid sharing materials and reduced the need for sanitation.

Appropriate clothing makes or breaks outdoor learning experiences in four-season climates. To address the gear gap, PPS purchased 500 hats and gloves, snow pants for elementary students, and many bolts of fleece to make lap blankets and neck gaiters.

The funding came primarily from money received by the district from the federal CARES Act, and from grants from the Foundation for Portland Public Schools, as well as in-kind donations of time and materials from the community. To further support the transition to outdoor learning, PPS created a stipend building liaison position for each school. The building liaisons coordinated material distribution, infrastructure installation, and communications with teachers about schedules and curricular opportunities. They also recruited volunteers and secured additional in-kind donations for outdoor building materials and supplies.

The district recognized that their teachers needed additional support to move their usual curriculum from an indoor model to one that could take place outside. In the summer prior to school opening, in collaboration with local partners, they created a professional development video to provide faculty with initial strategies, tips, and advice about how to teach outside.

As teachers settled into their outdoor classroom spaces in the fall, PPS added to their professional development program. They are now shifting their focus to enable and encourage teachers to continue outdoor learning as a permanent addition to their long-term instructional model for the district.

Conclusion

Many will look back on this period and feel a gut punch. We get that and acknowledge the impacts that the 2020–2021 school year has had on the education system as a whole and especially students. The goal of all of us as educators was to identify the most pressing needs of students and cater instruction to meet those needs. Many students achieved academic growth during this time because they were provided with access, resources, and tools for learning that kept them connected and engaged.

We think education will emerge from this challenging time changed forever but stronger than ever. Educators found ways to approach difficult situations with innovative thinking, creativity, and empathy. In this book, we'll use our experiences prior to and amidst the pandemic to help you reimagine learning for your classroom. The strategies, recommendations, and ideas provided in this book will not only be useful for crisis scenarios but are also designed to be effective no matter what learning environment you're teaching in or leading in.

 ## Reflecting for Professional Growth

- What aspects of teaching were most challenging during the pandemic?

- What tools and strategies did you find successful during the pandemic?

- What new instructional strategies did you discover during the pandemic that you plan to carry forward?

- How will you close the learning gap created by an interruption of learning during the pandemic?

- Why is a focus on personalized learning more critical than ever before?

CHAPTER 2

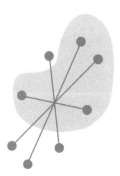

Planning Essentials for Blended Learning and Beyond

Outcomes for Professional Learning

In this chapter, we'll discuss:

- Exploring blended learning models
- Planning and integrating actions for blended learning success
- Assessing blended learning readiness

CONNECTING TO THE ISTE STANDARDS FOR EDUCATORS

The content of this chapter relates to the following indicators:

Designer (2.5.a) Educators use technology to create, adapt and personalize learning experiences that foster independent learning and accommodate learner differences and needs.

Designer (2.5.b) Educators design authentic learning activities that align with content area standards and use digital tools and resources to maximize active, deep learning.

Designer (2.5.c) Educators explore and apply instructional design principles to create innovative digital learning environments that engage and support learning.

Facilitator (2.6.a) Educators foster a culture where students take ownership of their learning goals and outcomes in both independent and group settings.

Facilitator (2.6.b) Educators manage the use of technology and student learning strategies in digital platforms, virtual environments, hands-on makerspaces or in the field.

Analyst (2.7.a) Educators provide alternative ways for students to demonstrate competency and reflect on their learning using technology.

During the pandemic, we all experienced varying degrees of online and blended learning. As we continue reimagining learning going forward, classrooms will definitely include some form of blended learning. This chapter examines the various models of blended learning to help you better understand what they might look like in your classroom and to ensure that you have the necessary design essentials to implement blended learning in your school.

Keep in mind that the models discussed here are not prescriptive, and many schools combine aspects of multiple models to create something entirely unique. One common theme is that every blended learning model requires varying degrees of technology use and implementation. So, if you're a school leader interested in growing blended learning, be sure the model you're considering pairs well with your available device and infrastructure resources, teacher-developed content, and the amount of professional development support you're able to provide.

Exploring Blended Learning Models

The Clayton Christensen Institute has identified the following seven blended learning models (2021):

- Station Rotation
- Lab Rotation
- Individual Rotation
- Flipped Classroom
- Flex
- A La Carte
- Enriched Virtual

Each model is unique and offers a variety of tools to meet your students' learning needs. Let's take a closer look at each of the seven models.

Model #1: Station Rotation

According to the Christensen Institute, "The Station Rotation model allows students to rotate through stations on a fixed schedule, where at least one of the stations is an online learning station. This model is most common in elementary schools because teachers are already familiar with rotating in 'centers' or stations" (2021). Station Rotation allows you to create personalized learning experiences for students and support individual students in need of additional support. For example, students might complete a skills lesson review, a reading activity, an individualized task or assignment, or an online assessment to determine current performance levels. The power of this model is the power to personalize learning.

Model #2: Lab Rotation

The Lab Rotation model is similar to the Station Rotation model because it "allows students to rotate through stations on a fixed schedule. However, in this case, online learning occurs in a dedicated computer lab. This model allows for flexible scheduling arrangements with teachers and other paraprofessionals, and it enables schools to make use of existing computer labs" (Clayton Christensen Institute, 2021). Like Station Rotation, this model also allows for personalization.

Model #3: Individual Rotation

"The Individual Rotation model," the Christensen Institute states, "allows students to rotate through stations, but on individual schedules set by a teacher or software algorithm. Unlike other rotation models, students do not necessarily rotate to every station; they rotate only to the activities scheduled on their playlists" (2021). What makes this model different from the others? It's the student experience. Each day the student is given a road map of which stations to work in. Station assignments are determined based upon the student's unique learning needs. Like Station Rotation and Lab Rotation, the experience is personalized.

Model #4: Flipped Classroom

As the Christensen Institute describes it, "The Flipped Classroom model flips the traditional relationship between class time and homework. Students learn at home via online coursework and lectures, and teachers use class time for teacher-guided practice or projects. This model enables teachers to use class time for more than delivering traditional lectures" (2021). It also allows for practice and application to happen at school with the support and help of a teacher. Moreover, this model offers high levels of engagement, as students remain active during class.

Model #5: Flex

"The Flex model lets students move on fluid schedules among learning activities according to their needs. Online learning is the backbone of student learning in a Flex model. Teachers provide support and instruction on a flexible, as-needed basis while students work through course curriculum and content," explains the Christensen Institute (2021). This model can give students a high degree of control over their learning. During the pandemic, many districts and schools offered in-person learning that represented the Flex model in action. Students accessed online course curriculum and content in the classroom, and teachers assisted them when they needed additional support. Moreover, teachers were able to closely monitor performance and pacing, working to ensure that all students were successful.

Model #6: A La Carte

The distinguishing feature of the A La Carte model is student access. This model "enables students to take an online course with an online teacher of record, in addition to other face-to-face courses, which often provides students with more flexibility over their schedules. A La Carte courses can be a great option when schools can't provide particular learning opportunities, such as an Advanced Placement or elective course, making it one of the more popular models in high schools" (Clayton Christensen Institute, 2021). In other words, the A La Carte model enables students to access and complete a course or courses not available at their schools. Some districts and schools utilize this as a strategy to provide equitable learning experiences for all students.

Model #7: Enriched Virtual

The Christensen Institute describes its final model, the Enriched Virtual model, as "an alternative to full-time online school that allows students to complete the majority of coursework online at home or outside of school, but attend school for required face-to-face learning sessions with a teacher. Unlike the Flipped Classroom, Enriched Virtual programs usually don't require daily school attendance; some programs may only require twice-weekly attendance, for example" (2021). This model is another practice that districts and schools experimented with during the pandemic. While most learning and assignments were online, students still had the opportunity of in-person learning, coaching, and support.

Selecting the Right Model

Each model or variation of a model affords varying degrees of student flexibility, voice, choice, responsibility, engagement, and so on. To select the appropriate model for you and your students, you will want to match the model to the student and teacher experience tailored for your school. In the following sections, we will outline effective blended learning essentials as a part of the teacher and student experience to help in making this determination.

STOP. REFLECT. PLAN. ACT.

Selecting the Right Blended Learning Model

Professional Learning Task. In this section, we discussed the various types of blended learning models. Take a moment to **stop**, **reflect**, **plan**, and **act**. Use the space below to answer the posed questions. This will help you assess which model is most appropriate for your classroom, school, or district.

What do you want students to control in the blended learning context?

What do you want teachers to control in the blended learning context?

Based upon your answers to the previous two questions, which blended learning model or models achieves the desired state for both of your answers?

Planning and Implementation Actions for Blended Learning Success

Through our work with districts and schools, we've identified critical actions associated with blended learning success. Those planning and implementation actions include:

- Identifying and deploying devices
- Establishing a digital infrastructure
- Managing the project
- Developing the foundation for professionals

- Preparing learners for success

- Managing student profiles and the environment

- Assigning tasks for student engagement

- Facilitating learning and learning environments

- Personalizing learning

- Growing professionals

In the next sections, we will examine each action in greater detail—offering a foundation for successfully planning and implementing your blended learning strategy.

Action #1: Identifying and Deploying Devices

Research shows that the most positive impacts on student learning result from effective 1:1 implementation. The key word there is *effective*. You've probably heard of short-sighted districts that purchased thousands of devices without a plan for how to utilize them or about districts that purchased devices that do not support teacher and student needs. Don't be one of these. When considering devices for your district, school, or classroom, think about a few key questions before purchasing anything (this action is particularly helpful for instructional designers):

- What value will the devices add?

- Are the devices easy for teachers to use and for students to learn?

- Will you be able to facilitate device training for teachers and students, or does the vendor provide professional development?

Will you implement a 1:1 program, where every student gets a device?

 Once you have decided on devices, the next step is to plan your deployment. To help you, we adapted the 5 Step Planning Process from Future Ready Schools (n.d.) into a checklist. Scan the QR code for a downloadable version.

IDENTIFYING AND DEPLOYING DEVICES CHECKLIST

◯ Reach out to the community to build awareness and support for your initiative.

◯ Collaborate with those responsible for professional development in the design and offering of personalized, multimodal training for students, parents, and teachers.

◯ Provide professional learning opportunities for administrators and other staff, as well as time for teachers to design lessons that leverage the use of the devices in learning.

◯ Build a technical support team (often involving students and teachers) and a help desk with the capacity to handle the added load of this device deployment.

◯ Establish and build the capacity of instructional coaches and other educational technology (ET) staff to provide ongoing supports.

◯ Establish professional learning networks (PLNs) that support educators, IT staff, ET staff, and others to exchange ideas and share lessons learned. Social media platforms (especially Twitter) can be a great place for this.

◯ Develop a three- to five-year budget that addresses the total cost of ownership of the devices across their anticipated life cycle, including replacement costs.

◯ Present the plan to the school board or appropriate subcommittees, with budget requests.

◯ Update responsible use policies and parent consent processes for the new device strategy.

◯ Create strategies for obtaining and funding insurance coverage for devices.

◯ Develop a digital citizenship curriculum and plan for implementation of the curriculum with all students.

◯ Create a deployment schedule that synchronizes all elements of the plan outlining the rollout.

◯ Create a strategy for developing the necessary instructional resources to transition to an emphasis on multimedia, multimodal learning.

◯ Develop metrics that include indicators and associated data collection for measuring progress, as well as a feedback loop for using this data to inform continuous improvement.

Action #2: Establishing a Digital Infrastructure

Establishing a sound digital infrastructure ensures that you are able to focus on what you do best: facilitating meaningful learning experiences. It goes beyond just ensuring there is proper bandwidth (speaking of, Chief Information Officers we've talked with always say to double the bandwidth you think you might need). High-quality and secure digital infrastructure systems within and outside of a school are essential to supporting anytime, anywhere learning and to advancing comprehensive blended learning.

Logistical support has always been important, even when using print resources. It's important to work with your district leadership team to create an information technology (IT) support team for the daily support needed by teachers and students. The IT support team must be proactive and provide training and resources to prepare teachers and students to leverage technology for learning, thereby reducing potential disruptions that might occur. Principals, teachers, and coaches should be trained to identify inequities that hinder students' blended learning experience, such as limited access to tools and resources outside of school. As more teachers and students leverage resources through devices, the logistics of technical services becomes more important, from initial access to ongoing support to teachers and students.

Action #3: Managing the Project

 Like logistics, managing the implementation (or a 1:1 project) is always important to ensuring a successful return on investment—learning, in this case. The quantity and complexity of steps involved in digitally enhanced learning transformations are prompting many to employ the principles of project management, including us. Scan the QR code for our checklist to help with your blended learning project management responsibilities.

BLENDED LEARNING PROJECT MANAGEMENT CHECKLIST

◯ Create a communication plan and status reporting process.

◯ Build an action plan with key tasks and a calendar with dates for completion.

◯ Order devices and appropriate software and appropriate apps.

◯ Create a training schedule and implement training.

◯ Coordinate delivery of devices and/or apps.

◯ Set up devices and/or apps.

◯ Coordinate data and identity.

◯ Create an evaluation plan to determine the return on investment.

◯ Report out the effectiveness of implementation.

Action #4: Developing a Foundation for Professional Development

Technology can enrich professional development (PD) when the technology itself is not the sole focus of the PD, but instead when it's leveraged to expand access to high-quality, enduring, job-embedded opportunities for professional learning among educators. These focused PD sessions can lead to improved learning outcomes, academic success, and increased digital literacy for our students who must thrive and learn in our digital world. PD enhanced with technology (online courses, in person, social media, and so on) can offer educators a multitude of opportunities to collaborate, learn, innovate, share, design, and nourish effective practices with colleagues across the country and even the globe. Before you begin planning PD implementation, you must first ensure the school culture embraces the idea that mistakes are often necessary for learning to occur. Create a safe environment in which teachers can go beyond their comfort levels, make and acknowledge mistakes, and learn from them. As you begin designing your PD plan, you can use the following checklist (or download a copy using the QR code) to ensure implementation of an effective professional development program.

PROFESSIONAL DEVELOPMENT PROGRAM IMPLEMENTATION CHECKLIST

- ◯ Embed practice time for new skills, apps, and tools for teachers.
- ◯ Embed practice time for new skills, apps, and tools for students.
- ◯ Provide time for sharing ideas, giving and receiving feedback respectfully, listening actively.
- ◯ Decide appropriate teachers and staff to attend trainings. The training for a principal or technology coach might not be the same training as for a teacher.
- ◯ Group educators accordingly. Sample configurations include grade level teams, content area teams, and interdisciplinary teams.
- ◯ Create a timeline for a series of professional development opportunities.
- ◯ Create a "messaging plan" describing the purpose of the new technology, device, or app.
- ◯ Frame the timing of the PD around the deployment of the device or technology. Begin it during the planning phase, continue during implementation with students, and schedule just-in-time training throughout the year.
- ◯ Specify how many sessions will occur per year in your PD implementation plan. The number may vary depending on cohort, classroom, or school building.
- ◯ Align the master schedule to allow teachers to have time together.
- ◯ Leverage existing professional development time and staff meetings.
- ◯ Transform faculty meetings and use them for professional learning, not information dissemination.
- ◯ Use rotating subs.
- ◯ Use time when students are meeting: community circles, pep rallies, plays, assemblies, performances.
- ◯ Collaborate with staff to develop and use agreed-upon norms to build trust and ensure balanced participation during meetings.
- ◯ Provide feedback in a manner that makes the colleagues feel safe. Use sentence stems such as "I like..." and "I wonder..."
- ◯ Develop, communicate, and model shared language expectations around your implementation.

Even though the purpose of the professional development plan is to improve teaching and learning, there must be a very clear and concise portion of the training dedicated to how to actually use the device. Educators must be able to use the device or app in a blended learning environment, informed by sound pedagogy and strategies. Be sure that the device or technology offers ongoing support, coaching, and collaboration. If it does not, this is something you or your IT leadership team will want to ensure is a part of the implementation plan.

To optimally impact personalization and student growth, teacher practices must also evolve. With this in mind, throughout the book we highlight many pedagogical approaches, strategies, and practices to support educators, no matter what device or app is being implemented. Many of these transcend the blended learning environment and are effective in various learning environments.

Action #5: Preparing Learners for Success

Thus far we've focused on infrastructure and planning but not so much on what actually happens in the classroom. The end goal of planning is to prepare learners for success. We all must collaboratively design—and in an ongoing improvement process, redesign—what classrooms of the future look like, ensuring that we're responsive to the needs of our learners. Often in education we find ourselves responding to societal, economic, and global pressures. During the pandemic, we teachers even shifted our profession to a remote environment to respond to the educational needs of learners. Instead of responding, what if education was the primary influencer and innovator in bringing about progressive change? As teachers, that begins by understanding and planning for learner success. Consider the following list of questions as you begin planning and preparing for learner success in your classroom.

PLANNING FOR LEARNER SUCCESS

- As a teacher, are you a lifelong learner?
- Have you unpacked the learning standards in your grade level or content level, and do you truly understand the level of thinking complexity that students must demonstrate?
- How does the technology you're implementing shape students' thinking?
- How can students use technology to shape their own thinking?

- Do you have a process for collecting and organizing resources?

- Have you conducted an inventory of your students' interests and readiness for blended learning? Which model most appropriately meets the present needs of your students?

- Have you organized your digital learning space?

- Have you organized your physical learning space?

- What do you want learners to be able to do when the lesson is over?

- What does mastery look like for that day?

- What is one way your classroom has changed recently?

- How are you planning to change in the near future?

- How could your classroom's physical setup change to more optimally contribute to success with blended learning?

- Can you eliminate a teacher desk? Why or why not?

- What does your workspace outside the classroom look like?

Action #6: Integrating Students into the Learning Environment and LMS

For decades, learning management and classroom management have been a part of the physical classroom experience. A well-functioning classroom is a prerequisite for high-quality instruction and high levels of student engagement. This is true for blended instruction and learning too.

Signposts of a well-functioning classroom include effective use of instructional groups and seamless transitions that are completed efficiently. The digital learning environment must receive the same kind of attention and focus as a physical learning space. In the blended environment, much of this focus and attention centers on the learning management system (LMS). An LMS is an application or tool, typically web-based, used for delivering instruction to students. An LMS also offers administrative features for teachers such as documentation, tracking, reporting, and more.

For blended learning success, teachers must establish and monitor routines and procedures to ensure the smooth operation of the blended classroom and the LMS—and teach students to feel confident using all the digital resources available to them. This is the foundation for a student-directed blended learning classroom.

The following list of questions can guide you and help ensure that you are preparing for and integrating students into the blended environment successfully.

MANAGING LEARNING PROFILES AND ENVIRONMENTS

- How many digital applications and technologies will be implemented in each classroom?

- Is the LMS highly integrated and can it be used to connect to other digital applications and technologies used in the classroom?

- Do you have digital applications that will monitor, manage, and filter any school device on your network?

- Do you have digital applications to automate time-consuming and tedious administrative tasks, like maintaining classroom rosters, so that you can optimize your time and focus on instruction?

- Which digital applications allow you to collect user progression and activity data to ensure students are fully engaged in learning?

- Do you have appropriate digital storage?

- Will students be able to collaborate on assignments and projects using digital applications and technologies?

- Will you (as a teacher) be able to grade and provide feedback to students virtually?

Action #7: Assigning Tasks for Student Engagement

One of the many benefits of teaching online is that you can automate communications to students and the distribution of assignments and tasks to students. There are also many other tools of engagement, allowing you to differentiate, personalize, and individualize your instruction in ways that aren't possible in the physical classroom. This is part of the magic of blended learning—using the best tools and resources from online learning—and bringing them to the brick-and-mortar classroom. As you begin considering how to engage students in the blended classroom, use the following questions to guide your practice.

ENGAGING STUDENTS IN DIGITAL ENVIRONMENTS

- Have you identified and prioritized the learning tasks that all students should master?

- Have you ensured that tasks align to the level of rigor required by the standard?

- Have you clearly defined what mastery performance indicators look like?

- Are you explicitly teaching and modeling the habits and skills that you want your students to use online (communication etiquette, timelines for assignments, and so on)?

- Have you prepared and planned for differentiated supports, because some students will need additional time and alternative supports?

- Have you planned for enrichment activities and how they will be distributed to students?

- Have you adopted tools and created tasks that assess student mastery of learning?

- Have you adopted tools that allow you to provide academic feedback in relation to outcomes for student learning?

- Have you adopted tools that allow for personalized paths and playlists?

- Have you ensured assignments are authentic and mirror the real world?

- Have you adopted tools that allow you to record and easily send instructional videos to your students?

When students have digital access, the learning tasks can evolve in ways not possible in the physical classroom. With the right digital tool, for example, students are able to receive feedback from their teacher and their peers, and then revise and improve their work easily with the right digital tool. Whatever digital tools you select to engage students, the work must still be grounded in moving students along their learning journey and providing meaningful reflection and enrichment opportunities.

Action #8: Facilitating Learning and Learning Environments

Deep levels of student learning of both concepts and digital age skills require more than just well-defined digital infrastructure and learning platforms. We must also continuously improve our pedagogies and adapt strategies to student needs.

Engagement with problem-solving and critical thinking is enhanced through improvements to design and pedagogies. According to Hattie (2009), two actions have a significant, positive effect on student achievement: the teacher's ability to guide learning through classroom interactions and the ability to monitor learning and provide feedback. Let's apply the same effective, research-based thinking to blended instruction as we do to traditional brick-and-mortar instruction. To help you get started, we've highlighted a few instructional practices that are enhanced by blended learning.

ENHANCING INSTRUCTIONAL PRACTICES WITH BLENDED LEARNING

Student Metacognition. Metacognition is thinking about one's thinking. In the traditional classroom this could be done live in person, in a small group, or through a pencil and paper activity. But many times, the emotion felt by a student is lost through the traditional approach. In a blended environment, have students record themselves as they explain a process to capture their tone and body language while they express their thinking. The focus of this activity is more on the thinking process than on explicitly providing step-by-step directions on how to do something.

Modeling/Think-Aloud. The purpose of a think-aloud is not to illuminate that there is only one way, only one right way, or one perfect way of doing something. It's also not to point to careless mistakes or erroneous reasoning (thinking process). Think-alouds allow students to observe how successful individuals navigate and negotiate social and functional environments, and this can easily be adapted to the blended setting. In a blended classroom, try reasoning out loud while recording yourself and purposefully include natural errors in your thought process.

Day-in-the-Life Scenarios. During day-in-the-life scenarios, students engage in interactive explorations of scenarios in which they imagine they are a character in a book, a person in history, or a thing (like an electron). In a blended environment, students can collectively problem-solve, brainstorm ideas, consider options, check the viability of solutions, and describe the why behind an agreed-upon solution using synchronous and asynchronous digital chatting tools. In addition, the finished product can be a "film" documenting the day in the life scenario.

Dissecting Exemplars. Students analyze exemplars and reflect upon why the solution is successful while also considering other positive alternatives. In a blended environment, this can be done in-person, during a synchronous class session, or even asynchronously using online collaboration tools.

Dissecting Non-Examples. Students analyze non-examples, dissect errors, and generate scenarios that could turn these non-examples into exemplars.

Small Group. During small-group instruction, teachers model thinking and possible solution paths, and students ask questions, communicate their thinking, and produce their solutions in various forms: live in person, in writing, synchronous video (through small group video conferencing breakout rooms), or visually through recorded videos. All of the formats and modes of sharing student work make small groups ideal for blended learning.

Application. Students apply new knowledge or skills to tasks, projects, and learning situations. Learning experiences are crafted in ways that allow students control of the path and pace. Blended learning environments allow for students to apply new learning in asynchronous online/offline mediums, online collaborative mediums, and even in-person collaborative mediums.

Checking for Understanding and Feedback. Teachers and peers provide timely and specific feedback to help students reflect on the processes that led to solutions, and the solution itself. Students also self-assess their solutions using a rubric that has been co-created and shared prior to the project or lesson. In the blended setting, checks for understanding can be administered through quick online response forms, an LMS, question prompts, video conferences, exit tickets, in-person conversations, and so on. This allows for more personalized pathways for formative assessment. Data collected through digital means also allows teachers to leverage analytics to target supports more easily.

Many times, educators perceive that when they switch to a blended learning model, interactive whole group experiences no longer occur. Actually, the opposite is true; blended learning allows for richer and more meaningful whole group learning experiences. Because blended learning incorporates online and in-person experiences, learners can access resources at their own pace and tackle concepts and build skills in the way that best fits their schedule, motivation, needs, and strengths. Blended learning is also much more efficient because learners benefit from direct instruction or working with peers, instead of wasting time on task instructions or transitioning from activity to activity.

Elements of the blended learning space support and foster personalized learning. No matter what blended learning model you're using, the structure of learning time and student grouping must be flexible, responsive to student needs, and based on formative assessment data. Reflecting on the following list of questions can help ensure that you are continuing to engage students in flexible learning environments.

CONTINUING ENGAGEMENT IN FLEXIBLE LEARNING ENVIRONMENTS

- Have you developed, taught, and reinforced classroom procedures and digital citizenship?

- Do students take charge of the pace and the path of their learning?

- Do you regularly check and ensure digital assets are accessible and are properly linked?

- Do you have a process for grouping students into learning teams?

- Do students know what it takes to demonstrate success in the classroom?

- Does the learning environment illuminate each student's voice?

- Are you using data walls (brick-and-mortar or virtual) to individualize and personalize learning for your students?

Once you establish a structure and routine, you can be more confident about relinquishing control and empowering students to take charge of their learning. As a blended learning teacher, you have embraced risk-taking, are bold, and empower students to take charge of their learning.

Action #9: Personalizing Learning

The concept of personalized learning has been around for some time, but the adoption of personalized learning approaches has increased significantly with the quick transition to remote and hybrid learning ushered in because of the pandemic. During that time, many edtech tools made rapid advances in their platforms and digital content to better meet the needs of schools. Although there is not yet one shared definition of personalized learning, leading practitioners in the field generally look for an approach that supports:

- Tailoring instruction to each student's individual strengths, needs, skills, interests, and aspirations (sometimes captured in a personalized learning plan)

- A variety of rich learning experiences that allow for student agency or voice and choice

- Increasing focus on the teachers' integral role as a facilitator of student learning (instead of an imparter of knowledge)

When designing personalized learning experiences, pay attention not only to designing instructional tasks but also to designing flexible and robust learning environments, providing students with expert guidance and support while increasing their ownership of learning.

There are many models and strategies that are characterized as personalized learning, but for understanding and demonstration purposes we will be focusing on two specific strategies: Personalized Learning Pathways, which are commonly called playlists, and Competency Based Progression, which is also referred to as master-based learning.

Playlists

Playlist creation is exactly like curating your favorite songs in your music app to create different groupings of songs that suit your various moods or activities. Similarly, teachers use playlists based on assessment data to address students' learning needs, including readiness, interest, and background knowledge. Teachers begin with a unit, standard, objective, or outcome for learning, and then break it down into a series of learning tasks. Tasks are meaningfully curated based on the differentiated needs of students. Students then receive access to a playlist to complete the tasks, ideally with the flexibility of choosing where to start and what order to proceed through the tasks. Playlist access is provided through technological means, which further facilitates assessment and differentiation as it allows teachers to monitor performance quickly and create or adjust tasks accordingly.

There are some great digital tools available that make planning playlist-based instruction easy. Many LMSs can help you differentiate based on student needs or student choices. Instead of listening to the teacher lecture on the phases of the cell division cycle, for example, students could choose from different activities that explain it. You could post a Khan Academy video or teacher-created video that highlights the cycle with annotations, or create a short video that you record yourself and share your screen with visuals and animations. Next students might have a series of prompts or tasks in their playlist that are tailored to their academic needs. These could be based on their current reading level, previous formative assessment, or personal learning profile. To better understand this concept, consider the following example playlist for a ninth-grade biology mitosis lesson.

NINTH-GRADE BIOLOGY MITOSIS LESSON

Teacher Directions: Post a scenario on Google Classroom (or your district LMS).

Student Directions: You fell off your bike and scuffed your knee. A few days later your scab peeled off, and there is new skin there. How does that happen? Reply to the thread.

Teacher Directions: On Seesaw (or your district LMS), post the Khan Academy link to Mitosis.

Student Directions: Click the hyperlink to watch a video on Mitosis.

Student Directions: Open a jam in Google Jamboard and create a model of the cell division process. Feel free to use shapes or your own drawings. Don't forget to annotate your model.

Student Directions: Progress through the Google Jamboard jams and write three sticky notes to place on other students' jams, providing feedback on their models.

Student Directions: Using a video creation tool, create an instructional video of the cell cycle for your classmates. Write a script in Google Docs describing what is happening at each stage of the cell cycle. Post your videos on Seesaw.

It is important to remember that creating and implementing playlists is an iterative process. You might find students are skipping or waiting until the last minute to complete certain tasks. You might want to gather feedback as to why this is the case and make modifications as needed. You might also design variations of the playlist depending on where students are in their learning journeys. Taking the mitosis lesson as an example, students who have already mastered the phases of cell division could choose to engage in a chicken coop project, taking mitosis further, into genetic inheritance. When the eggs arrive, students might research the types of eggs received and begin incubation. Students could then monitor the daily conditions in the incubator and begin designing a coop for when the chickens hatch. This task helps students understand cell division, Deoxyribonucleic Acid (DNA), and inheritance. As comfort and proficiency are achieved, students potentially could co-design the playlists with you.

Competency-Based Learning Progressions

In the personalized learning strategy of competency-based learning progressions, each student's progress toward clearly defined goals is continually assessed, and assessment occurs "on demand" when a student is ready to demonstrate competency. Assessment can take a variety of forms, such as projects or presentations, as well as more traditional selected response instruments. A student advances through the content at their own pace and earns course credit (if applicable) as soon as he or she demonstrates a mastery level of competency, rather than waiting until the end of the term or school year.

As a national leader in competency-based education, the state of Vermont has adopted flexible and personalized pathways, requiring students to progress and graduate based on mastery of skills and knowledge. Vermont sets the competencies expected for graduation and performance indicators to map out that trajectory. To measure student learning along their tailored paths, the state developed guidelines for task models and scoring criteria, emphasizing transferable skills that link the classroom to real world application. With these expectations and supports, Vermont districts and schools possess the autonomy for determining the best models for their students—a truly personalized approach to learning.

FROM THE FIELD

Champlain High School

Champlain Valley Union High School in Hinesburg, Vermont, began implementing proficiency-based learning in 2010. The focus was (and is) on how well students can demonstrate specific skills using the course content, instead of just on the content alone. Here are some examples of how this particular school used proficiency-based learning.

Example 1: K-U-D (Know, Understand, and Do) Chart

In a ninth-grade humanities course, teachers develop a K-U-D chart for the yearlong course, specifying what they want students to know, what they want students to understand, and what they want students to be able to do by the end of the course. That chart includes the topics students will study and the literature they will use, as well as twelve outcomes for student learning: skills including critical thinking, making and supporting a claim, as well as writing organization. Each of the twelve outcomes has a four-point rubric, or learning scale, that explicitly communicates what students need to do to show proficiency. Each outcome is designed to provide evidence that students are meeting one of the school's fourteen proficiency-based graduation standards. All of the high school's learning outcomes are transferable, meaning they are skills that can be applied across courses and discipline areas. For example, making and supporting a claim and critical thinking are skills that students can apply not just in humanities, but in science, math, history, and beyond the classroom.

Example 2: Evidence of the Learning Outcome

Students work on "evidence" for the learning outcome, which calls for using multiple, relevant, and specific pieces of evidence to develop and support a claim. Individually or in pairs, students identify topics they want to study in greater depth and begin their research. A graphic organizer can be provided to help students answer specific questions and organize new information for clarity and understanding.

At the bottom of the chart, the learning scale for evidence of the learning outcome shares what students must do to achieve a 1, 2, 3, or 4, providing students with a clear pathway for achieving the outcome and providing teachers with a rubric to evaluate students' work. By breaking down the standards into learning outcomes, teachers can pinpoint students' specific areas of learning and growth and then personalize instruction to help address individual needs. Learning scales are effective because they clearly identify the evidence to meet or exceed each outcome for student learning.

Example 3: Design Challenges

In another class, students are tasked with identifying a problem or issue in the school, then designing a project to address it. Students' projects range from making a mobile cart with yoga mats to organizing a breakfast club where students can discuss mental health issues to creating a podcast for the NPR Student Podcast Challenge. As students work to implement their diverse projects, all students are being assessed on the same four outcomes: evaluation, synthesis, iterative process, and media production and use.

Differentiation

Personalized learning also promotes differentiation, a process by which teachers proactively plan varied approaches to what students need to learn, how they will learn it, and how they will demonstrate mastery (Tomlinson, 1999). Some students learn at different rates and respond to different instructional approaches or strategies. Most educators have seen this in person, so differentiation in the brick-and-mortar classroom has been well-defined. Now that the world has changed and learning environments have shifted, we must also apply differentiated practices in the blended learning space. Blended learning provides students more choices in their learning by differentiating content, process, and/or product. Blended learning also offers opportunities for students to determine the place, the path, and the pace to achieve the intended outcome. This provides an opportunity to scale differentiation for all your student learners.

Action #10: Growing Professionals

Another essential action for blended learning success is growing professional practice. This isn't always easy as many teachers are repulsed by the words professional development or PD. It's not because teachers don't want to learn or grow, but that PD is frequently implemented in ineffective ways. For example, many PD offerings look like the standard one-size-fits-all format, where every teacher in the building is asked to report to the library and listen to an expert speak—exactly the instructional practice that's becoming outdated in classrooms. Even more disappointing is that the one-size-fits-all PD format is antithetical to the differentiated nature and approach to blended learning.

It's important to note that singular, occasional, episodic, periodic, and disconnected PD with limited to no connection to one another have little chance of producing substantial change or growth in teachers. These "events" may transmit information and raise awareness about blended learning but will not ignite lasting change or growth in practice. For blended learning to succeed, you must have practical, ongoing, progressive PD that is differentiated and that is tailored to the needs of teachers.

For teachers to adopt blending learning practices as well as thrive, it's critical that PD is designed with the adult learner in mind. To help bring this conceptional idea to life, we've come up with these four simple PD recommendations:

Recommendation 1. Teachers should be involved in the planning and in the evaluation of their learning (PD).

Recommendation 2. Learning (PD) should be problem-centered rather than content-oriented.

Recommendation 3. Blended learning experiences should be the basis for learning (PD) activities.

Recommendation 4. Learning (PD) should have immediate relevance and impact on teacher practice.

These recommendations are easy to implement, are cost neutral and don't require funding to execute, and are grounded in high-yield strategies for the adult learner. If you design blended learning PD with these recommendations in mind, PD will be practical, valuable, and impactful for your teachers.

So what might this look like in practical application? To answer that question, let's examine two approaches that are directly aligned with the PD recommendations as well as blending learning.

Collective Wisdom

Collective wisdom is a protocol used to tap into the collective expertise of all teachers when solving a problem or designing new instructional strategies or blended learning approaches. This protocol leverages the combined knowledge of all teachers—acknowledging and valuing the expertise, the experience, and the skills of teachers. Collective wisdom is also the grounding idea for professional learning communities (PLCs) or communities of practice. PLCs offer reoccurring cycles of collective inquiry and collective action where teachers collectively work to grow instructional practice.

One emerging collective wisdom strategy is the Pineapple Chart, a system that allows teachers to invite one another into their classrooms for informal observations. The Pineapple Chart is set up in a common location in the school that teachers frequent daily, such as the teacher's lounge, or online in an LMS community board, teacher Facebook group, or shared Google document. On the Pineapple Chart, teachers "advertise" the interesting things they are doing in classrooms and activities and practices they think other teachers might want to observe. Some examples of instructional activities that other teachers might want to observe include a STEM project, a history debate, a Zoom session with students from another part of the world, a read-aloud, and so on.

When you see something of interest on the chart, you go to that classroom at the designated time, sit down in an out-of-the-way spot, and just simply observe and learn. There is no expectation or requirement, no script to write or debriefing required. It's a no-stakes visit where you get to observe for as short or as long as you'd like what's happening in that teacher's class. These collective wisdom "Pineapple Visits" are effective ways for teachers to learn new skills and techniques just when they need them. Moreover, this practice offers agency with teachers self-selecting opportunities for growth and experiencing individualized professional learning based upon those needs.

Unconferences, Edcamps, and PLNs

One popular version of the unconference is the Edcamp. Edcamps, according to founder Digital Promise, are free public events that leverage the knowledge and experiences of teachers by allowing educators to collaboratively determine topics for discussion the day of the event. Teachers facilitate sessions by using their experiences to drive conversation with their peers. To maximize impact, educators are encouraged to find Edcamp sessions that best meet their professional learning needs.

According to Digital Promise (2021), Edcamps are centered around these core tenets:

Free and Open to All. Open to educators of all grade levels, Edcamps are always presented as free to attendees.

Participant Driven. Unlike traditional conferences, Edcamps do not have predetermined topics. Participants collaboratively decide on the topics, which are finalized on the day of in-person events. Online Edcamp topics are collectively sourced during the registration phase to ensure an efficient use of the online time.

Experience, not Experts. Edcamps are about the collective wisdom of the participants, not about flown-in experts giving a keynote or session.

Maximize Learning. Edcamps encourage participants to find sessions that meet their needs so they can get the most of the experience. If you are in a session that is not meeting your needs, you're encouraged to move on to another session that may be better suited for you.

Vendor Free. Edcamps pride themselves on being grassroots and vendor-free. No purchasing of services required.

Unconferences, such as Edcamps, provide meaningful opportunities for teachers from all over the country to support one another, identify and discuss similar challenges and solutions, as well as amplify best teaching practices and resources. Blended learning encompasses so many different learning contexts, and it's important to build community among other educators dedicated to engaging students with this powerful practice. Purposeful community building is also the idea behind professional learning networks (PLNs).

PLNs allow teachers to collaboratively reflect on experiences together through social media platforms, such as Twitter, Facebook Groups, Voxer, WhatsApp, and more. PLNs increase teacher confidence and competence with the (digitally enhanced) learning transformation. There is so much power in a PLN, as it allows teachers to learn from mentors, coaches, and leaders from across the globe. A PLN can serve as your go-to group of educators, based upon your interests, passions, and areas you'd like to grow. For context, the following graphic lists the goals of a PLN.

GOALS OF A PLN

- Inspire new ideas
- Push your thinking
- Share resources and ideas
- Support you through challenges
- Celebrate successes together
- Serve as your daily dose of positivity and humor
- Provide on-demand PD
- Ask questions to help you reflect on practice
- Build relationships on a personal level

How are you taking the successes and lessons learned in your blended classroom and building the collective wisdom of others? If you are a school leader, how are you designing PD in a way that leverages the experiences, talents, and expertise of your teachers? As you begin considering and designing PD for the blended learning context, don't forget to engage and tap into the talents of your teachers. Teachers listen to other teachers. Engaging teachers in creating, designing, and delivering PD for blended learning is a great way to create ownership and buy-in—so start from the ground up.

Conclusion

In this chapter, we provided a planning framework (consisting of planning essentials) so that you can create a blended learning experience that best meets the needs of your district, school, or classroom. You might also use the framework as a means of getting support from decision makers in your district or school. No matter which model you chose, there must be conditions and structures in place to fulfill the innovative potential of the school. Planning requires visionary leaders who have both a personal passion for blended learning and a green light from the district to improve how they meet students' needs. Scaling blended learning also demands engaging and leveraging teachers in growing instructional practice. The planning essentials presented in this chapter are meant to support you in that journey.

Reflecting for Professional Growth

- Of the planning essentials you explored, which area needs the most work for your particular context?

- Who must you enlist to lead an effective blended learning rollout and subsequent implementation?

- What aspects of the design planning essentials do you want students to control? Which elements do you plan to manage yourself?

- What is the teacher's role in the successful implementation of blended learning?

CHAPTER 3

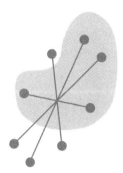

Mapping the Course Scope and Sequence

Outcomes for Professional Learning

In this chapter, we'll discuss:

- Formulating course objectives
- Creating outcomes for student learning
- Organizing and sequencing units and lessons
- Designing and aligning assessments with outcomes for student learning

CONNECTING TO THE ISTE STANDARDS FOR EDUCATORS

The content of this chapter relates to the following indicators:

Designer (2.5.c) Educators explore and apply instructional design principles to create innovative digital learning environments that engage and support learning.

Analyst (2.7.b) Educators use technology to design and implement a variety of formative and summative assessments that accommodate learner needs, provide timely feedback to students and inform instruction.

Analyst (2.7.c) Educators use assessment data to guide progress and communicate with students, parents and education stakeholders to build student self-direction.

During the pandemic, we all experienced the importance of long-term content planning. When we quickly translated instruction to the remote learning environment, it became more important than ever to have the scope and sequence developed for each course. Thoughtfully mapping the scope and sequence ensured continuity and progression—throughout the term or school year—despite the upheaval. This is true for any learning environment—traditional, blended, and online. In fact, many of the planning practices are the same. Post-pandemic, long-term planning and beginning the term or school year with a clear plan should continue. You never know when you might need to pivot between learning environments—so planning remains essential.

Extraordinary learning experiences don't happen by accident; they are intentionally designed by the teacher. As Lemov (2015) contended, "Begin with the end. Progress from unit planning to lesson planning. Define the objective, decide how you'll assess it, and then choose appropriate lesson activities" (p. 132). Don't worry, we are here to help with this process.

Long-term content planning involves a universal series of design steps or actions. Planning begins with mapping the course scope and sequence and ends with constructing aligned assessments. In this chapter we present a framework for mapping the scope and sequence. Our framework includes the following phases of development:

- Formulating course objectives

- Creating outcomes for student learning

- Organizing and sequencing units and lessons

- Aligning assessments

To begin, you must identify the essential knowledge and the essential skills for your course. What should students demonstrate after exiting your class? The specified knowledge and skills for your course drive the development of objectives. Objectives serve as the foundation for creating outcomes for student learning—the next step in the framework. Once objectives and outcomes are complete, it is time to organize and chunk objectives and outcomes into units and lessons. You also need to consider the flow and sequencing of student learning. For instance, units and lessons should be logically sequenced and built upon the former. Finally, assessment alignment must take place. It is imperative to have alignment between course objectives, outcomes, learning, and assessments. This is the key to beginning with the end in mind. The sections that follow explore and expand upon each of the developmental phases, framing the construction of your next course scope and sequence.

Formulating Course Objectives

You can't begin developing lessons or choosing instructional materials if you haven't determined the purpose of the course. So that's where course creation begins—with formulating course objectives. Objectives are broad statements that communicate a wide range of knowledge and skill (task, process, or strategy). Consider what knowledge or skill students must demonstrate upon completing your course. Vai and Sosulski (2016) contended that "objectives outline goals for the teacher to reach in a learning segment" (p. 207). Objectives also share the focus of instruction and the direction of the learning experience for students. Well-formulated course objectives should attend to:

- Providing a clear purpose to focus student learning

- Serving as a foundation for crafting outcomes for student learning

- Guiding the creation and selection of lessons, activities, and materials

- Directing the development of an assessment plan

Think of objectives as guiding priorities for your course. In some instances, you may be working with existing course objectives and even learning outcomes may that were shared directly with you. In other instances, you might be expected to create your objectives, but don't worry. We've crafted several resources to help you, such as the following chart of design tips for formulating course objectives.

DESIGN TIPS FOR FORMULATING COURSE OBJECTIVES		
Design Tip #1	Broad	Objectives are broad statements about student learning.
Design Tip #2	Enduring	Objectives communicate enduring understandings (knowledge and skill).
Design Tip #3	Active Voice	Objectives are written in the active voice (using present, past, or future tense).
Design Tip #4	Student-Centered	Objectives are student-centered, describing what students will do as opposed to what teachers will do.
Design Tip #5	Cohesive, Related, and Distinct	Objectives are cohesive, related, and distinct from each other.
Design Tip #6	Aligned	Objectives are aligned with the learning outcomes for the course.
Design Tip #7	Limited	Objectives are limited to no more than six or seven statements.

So how do the design tips translate into practice? Let's look at some example course objectives for math:

Course Objective #1. Students demonstrate their knowledge of operations and algebraic thinking by interpreting and representing multiplication as a comparison.

Course Objective #2. Students generalize place value, demonstrating how to read and write numbers to 1,000,000 using standard form, word form, and expanded form.

Course Objective #3. Students demonstrate an understanding of fraction equivalence by reasoning about the size of the fractions, using a benchmark fraction to compare the fractions, or finding a common denominator.

Course Objective #4. Students articulate the relative sizes of measurement units within one system of units.

Course Objective #5. Students analyze and classify shapes based on the line and the angle types.

Is each objective broad, enduring, student-centered, and in the active voice? Take a moment to review the example objectives and design tips again. Can you find any opportunities to improve the objectives? If so, how did the tips on formulating objectives inform your "improvements?"

STOP. REFLECT. PLAN. ACT.

Selecting the Right Blended Learning Model

Professional Learning Task. In this section, you began defining course objectives. In addition, you explored tips for constructing your own objectives. Take a moment to **stop**, **reflect**, **plan**, and **act**. In your own words, craft an operational definition of a course objective to guide future planning and action.

Creating Outcomes for Student Learning

Creating learning outcomes is the next phase of our framework. *Learning outcomes* center around a change in the learner. As Vai and Sosulski (2016) explained, "Learning outcomes are stated in terms of what the learner will know or be able to do if he [or she] has successfully completed a unit. As such, they are learner-centered" (p. 207). So how do you develop learning outcomes, and what are the essentials to consider when you're creating outcomes? In this section, we'll clarify how to craft aligned, impactful outcomes for student learning.

There are several ways to develop learning outcomes, but we will focus on using the SMART Learning Outcome method. SMART outcomes are specific, measurable, achievable, related, and timely. The following chart presents the SMART method and outlines essentials for creating learning outcomes. (Scan the QR code for a downloadable version.)

SMART LEARNING OUTCOMES METHOD		
S	Specific	Learning outcomes are **specific**, written in the active voice, clearly and definitively communicating what students will achieve (Vai & Sosulski, 2016).
M	Measurable	Learning outcomes are **measurable**, allowing you to assess student knowledge or skill (task, process, or strategy) (Vai & Sosulski, 2016).
A	Achievable	Learning outcomes are **achievable** for students or attainable, possible to accomplish.
R	Related	Learning outcomes are directly **related** or aligned with course objectives (Vai & Sosulski, 2016).
T	Timely	Learning outcomes are **timely** and attainable within the span of the course.

Why write your learning outcomes in the active voice (using present, past, or future tense)? With active voice, the subject performs the action. Active voice also uses fewer words, allowing you to communicate information clearly and concisely.

When developing SMART learning outcomes, it's also critical to determine the level of understanding required for each outcome. When designing assessments, this ensures that the thinking levels presented in the learning outcomes align with the thinking levels being assessed. Bloom's Taxonomy (1956) and various adaptations are frequently used to frame outcomes for student learning.

In 1956, educational psychologist Benjamin Bloom developed a classification of levels of intellectual behavior important in learning. Bloom created this taxonomy for categorizing the levels of abstraction of questions that commonly occur in educational settings. Bloom identified a hierarchy of six levels that increased in complexity and abstraction—from the simple recall of facts, *knowledge*, to the highest order of thinking, *evaluation*. The taxonomy presents the following performance levels:

- Creating

- Evaluating

- Analyzing

- Applying

- Understanding

- Remembering

 Performance levels are thinking abilities and skills presented as a learning continuum (Bloom, 1956). For instance, *remembering* is a simple task, whereas *creating* is a complex task requiring higher-order thinking. The following chart presents Bloom's Taxonomy, as a learning continuum, including a list of action verbs organized by subcategory. Scan the QR code for a downloadable version.

BLOOM'S TAXONOMY AND ASSESSMENT DESIGN		
PERFORMANCE LEVEL	**BLOOM'S CATEGORY**	**ALIGNED ACTION VERBS AND ASSESSMENT STRATEGIES**
Highest-Order Thinking Skills (HOTS)	**Creating** is using knowledge or skill to develop or produce original products.	• Animating • Collaborating • Combining • Composing • Creating • Critiquing • Designing • Facilitating • Filming • Improving • Leading • Podcasting • Programming • Simulating • Solving

Continued

BLOOM'S TAXONOMY AND ASSESSMENT DESIGN		
PERFORMANCE LEVEL	BLOOM'S CATEGORY	ALIGNED ACTION VERBS AND ASSESSMENT STRATEGIES
	Evaluating is making judgments about knowledge or skill.	• Advising • Choosing • Comparing • Contrasting • Defending • Detecting • Editorializing • Estimating • Hypothesizing • Judging • Measuring • Predicting • Proposing • Relating • Rating
	Analyzing is drawing connections between new knowledge or skills and existing knowledge or skills.	• Diagraming • Experimenting • Forecasting • Hypothesizing • Imagining • Modeling • Outlining • Organizing • Structuring • Testing

Continued

BLOOM'S TAXONOMY AND ASSESSMENT DESIGN

PERFORMANCE LEVEL	BLOOM'S CATEGORY	ALIGNED ACTION VERBS AND ASSESSMENT STRATEGIES
	Applying is using knowledge or skill in new situations or problems.	• Charting • Displaying • Illustrating • Interviewing • Presenting • Producing • Reenacting • Sketching • Solving • Writing
	Understanding is comprehending and explaining knowledge or skill without relating to other knowledge or skill.	• Annotating • Presenting • Categorizing • Estimating • Journaling • Paraphrasing • Predicting • Reporting • Researching • Rewriting • Summarizing • Translating • Web Questing
Lowest-Order Thinking Skills (LOTS)	**Remembering** is recalling specific knowledge or skill.	• Arranging • Defining • Identifying • Listing • Matching • Ordering • Selecting • Summarizing

Remember that learning outcomes are student-centered, describing what the learner can do after completing the lesson. Frequently, learning outcomes are expressed as "I can" statements.

So how do you create a learning outcome? The following is a useful framework for constructing learning outcomes:

Learning Outcome = Context of Environment + Tool + "I can"
+ Aligned Verb + Conceptual Nouns

For example, here's a learning outcome for a third-grade science course created using our framework:

Learning Outcome = Using digital research and presentation technologies,
I can design and present solutions to reduce the impact of natural hazards
(fires, landslides, earthquakes, volcanic eruptions, and floods) on the environment.

As you can see, the context of the environment, the tool, the aligned verb, and the conceptual nouns frame the "I can" statement.

STOP. REFLECT. PLAN. ACT.

Creating Outcomes for Student Learning

Professional Learning Task. In this section, you examined strategies and practices for constructing outcomes for student learning. Take a moment to **stop**, **reflect**, **plan**, and **act**. Acting upon your new knowledge and using the framework, create a learning outcome for a current or future course.

So far, you've explored formulating course objectives and creating learning outcomes, but you might wonder how course objectives translate into learning outcomes. In short, course objectives serve as the *foundation* for developing learning outcomes. For instance, review the following third-grade science example. Be sure to examine the relationship between the course objective and the learning outcome.

ASSOCIATING COURSE OBJECTIVES AND LEARNING OUTCOMES	
COURSE OBJECTIVE	LEARNING OUTCOMES
Students will advance their understanding of the relationship between human activity and the earth.	• Using the discussion board, I can collaborate with other students, citing specific evidence and supporting details, on how natural hazards (fires, landslides, earthquakes, volcanic eruptions, floods) impact humans and the environment. • Using digital research and presentation technologies, I can design and present solutions to reduce the impact of natural hazards (fires, landslides, earthquakes, volcanic eruptions, and floods) on the environment.

 As you considered the relationship between the course objective and the learning outcomes, you likely noticed that the course objective is broad. On the other hand, the learning outcomes are narrow. Also notice that the learning outcomes encompass the course objective's particular knowledge and skills ("students will advance their understanding of the relationship between human activity and the Earth"). This is why course objectives are created first, and then learning outcomes stem from those statements. As you get acquainted with this process, the following chart can help you align course objectives with learning outcomes and capture this information as you engage in designing your blended course. You can scan the QR code for a downloadable version, as well.

COURSE OBJECTIVES AND LEARNING OUTCOMES TEMPLATE	
COURSE: *Insert Course Title*	
Course Objective: *Insert Course Objective*	**Aligned Learning Outcome(s)** • *Insert Learning Outcome* • *Insert Learning Outcome* • *Insert Learning Outcome*
Course Objective: *Insert Course Objective*	**Aligned Learning Outcome(s)** • *Insert Learning Outcome* • *Insert Learning Outcome* • *Insert Learning Outcome*
Course Objective: *Insert Course Objective*	**Aligned Learning Outcome(s)** • *Insert Learning Outcome* • *Insert Learning Outcome* • *Insert Learning Outcome*
Course Objective: *Insert Course Objective*	**Aligned Learning Outcome(s)** • *Insert Learning Outcome* • *Insert Learning Outcome* • *Insert Learning Outcome*

Organizing and Sequencing Units and Lessons

A person's working memory can retain only limited amounts of information at a time. As Marzano (2017) explained, "When information is new to students, they best process it in small, understandable increments. This is because learners can hold only small amounts of information in their working memories" (p. 30). Chunking information into smaller segments allows the brain to process information faster and retain information for extended periods. This strategy improves memory performance, which is why chunking is critical to the design process, no matter the learning environment—traditional, blended, or online.

The next phase of mapping a course's scope and sequence entails organizing (chunking) and sequencing objectives and outcomes into manageable units and lessons of study. Vai and Sosulsk (2016) described this process, noting, "Blocks of information are broken up or 'chunked' into incremental learning sections, segments, or steps as is appropriate to the subject matter" (p. 192). Marzano (2017) further deconstructed this process asserting, "The teacher chunks content into small, digestible bites for students. If presenting new declarative knowledge, checks comprise concepts and details that logically go together. If presenting new procedural knowledge, the chunks comprise steps in a process that go together" (p. 30). As Marzano explained, chunking is essential as this step breaks instruction into smaller, "digestible bites" making the learning manageable for students. For course construction purposes, chunking involves breaking and sequencing instruction and learning into units and lessons. In this section we will describe how to organize and sequence units and lessons.

Lemov (2015) expanded upon unit planning, sharing that "Unit planning means methodically asking how one day's lesson builds off the previous day's, how it prepares for the next day's and how these all fit into a larger sequence of objectives that lead to mastery" (p. 133). Lemov indicated that units are broad cohesive segments of instructional content composed of corresponding, sequential lessons that are presented in a linear fashion. As you begin organizing and sequencing objectives and learning outcomes into units and lessons of study, leverage the following design tips to guide this process.

DESIGN TIPS FOR ORGANIZING AND SEQUENCING UNITS AND LESSONS		
Design Tip #1	Grouping	Group similar or related course objectives and learning outcomes together.
Design Tip #2	Prioritizing	Prioritize your groupings based upon importance. Do so at the objective and outcome level. Consider which objectives and outcomes are primary and which are secondary. Rank your sets in this manner.
Design Tip #3	Progressing	Organize your groupings based upon the progression of instruction and learning. Do so at the objective and outcome level. For instance, foundational knowledge and skill must be presented before complex knowledge and skill is introduced. Foundational learning comes first, scaling to the more complex and challenging learning.

Continued

DESIGN TIPS FOR ORGANIZING AND SEQUENCING UNITS AND LESSONS		
Design Tip #4	Sequencing	Sequence your groupings into logical and coherent units and lessons of study.
Design Tip #5	Chunking	Chunk groupings into short, manageable units and lessons (Marzano, 2017).
Design Tip #6	Titling	Title unit and lesson groupings, being sure that each title is brief and concise. Additionally, make sure that each title appropriately frames the broad unit or lesson topic.

 Grouping, prioritizing, progressing, sequencing, chunking, and titling are critical as you begin forming units and lessons. If you are still struggling with this process, we've got you covered. In conjunction with the above tips, use the following scope and sequence template to begin mapping out your blended course. (For a downloadable version, scan the QR code.)

SCOPE AND SEQUENCE TEMPLATE	
COURSE: *Insert Course Title*	
Unit: *Insert Unit Title* • *Insert Course Objective* • *Insert Course Objective*	**Lesson:** *Insert Lesson Title* • *Insert Learning Outcome* • *Insert Learning Outcome* • *Insert Learning Outcome*
	Lesson: *Insert Lesson Title* • *Insert Learning Outcome* • *Insert Learning Outcome* • *Insert Learning Outcome*
	Lesson: *Insert Lesson Title* • *Insert Learning Outcome* • *Insert Learning Outcome* • *Insert Learning Outcome*

The information presented in this section should help as you begin organizing and sequencing course objectives and learning outcomes into logical, coherent units and lessons. If this process doesn't come easy at first, have no fear. Developing the scope and sequence for a course can be messy at first. That's absolutely normal. Remember, it's an art form requiring constant practice and refinement to develop this skill fully.

Aligning Assessments

Assessment design requires creating a series of learning experiences, including aligning assessments with course objectives and learning outcomes, to measure student learning. Earlier in the chapter, we discussed beginning with the end in mind (Lemov, 2015). When completing the design of your course, you should end with aligned assessments that evaluate mastery of the course objectives and learning outcomes. That's what beginning with the end in mind means. In this section, we will explore how to achieve this level of alignment.

As you remember, objectives guide the construction of learning outcomes. Likewise, learning outcomes drive the development of instruction and the design of assessments. Each lesson's assessment should align with the learning outcomes for that particular lesson. Each unit assessment should align with the course objectives and learning outcomes for that specific unit. Moreover, the culminating assessment should align with the objectives and outcomes for the entire course. Knowing this, after developing objectives, outcomes, units, lessons, and sequencing units and lessons, you can begin creating aligned course assessments.

In Chapter 7, "Engaging Students with Authentic Assessments," we will dive deeper into assessment creation. For now, however, keep the following design tips in mind when crafting assessment items and tasks that directly align with your outcomes for student learning.

DESIGN TIPS FOR CREATING ASSESSMENT ITEMS AND TASKS *(Adapted from Fisher & Frey, 2007)*		
Design Tip #1	Alignment	Is each item or task directly aligned to a learning outcome for the segment being assessed?
Design Tip #2	Performance	Does each item or task require students to demonstrate the performance level (Bloom's Taxonomy) identified in the corresponding outcome for learning?
Design Tip #3	Appropriateness	Is each item or task the most appropriate assessment strategy for the learning outcome being measured?
Design Tip #4	Clarity	Does each item or task present a clear and definite action to be performed by the student?
Design Tip #5	Conciseness	Is each item or task presented concisely in simple student-friendly language?
Design Tip #6	Challenge	Does each item or task provide an appropriate challenge for students?
Design Tip #7	Correctness	Does each item or task have an answer that can be agreed upon by the experts?
Design Tip #8	Soundness	Is each item or task free of errors and irrelevant cues?
Design Tip #9	Bias-Free	Is each item or task free of bias?

Notice in the above chart that each assessment item or task must align with a learning outcome for the lesson or unit being tested. Hence, if you cannot connect each assessment item or task with a learning outcome for that particular lesson or unit, you should omit the item or task. If it's not an outcome for learning, then the knowledge or skill shouldn't be assessed. From the design tips shared, you also likely noticed that each item or task requires students to demonstrate the performance level from Bloom's Taxonomy identified in the corresponding outcome for learning. Remember that Bloom's Taxonomy is a range of performance levels from simple, lower-order thinking skills (or LOTS) to more complex, higher-order thinking skills (or HOTS).

As you begin designing assessments, remember that the action verb listed within an outcome for student learning also serves as the foundation for developing the assessment item or task. Also remember that the action verb comes from Bloom's Taxonomy and indicates the level of understanding or performance required of your students. As an example, let's review our previous learning outcome for third-grade science:

> **Learning Outcome = Using digital research and presentation technologies,**
> **I can design and present solutions to reduce the impact of natural hazards**
> **(fires, landslides, earthquakes, volcanic eruptions, and floods) on the environment.**

Can you identify action verbs aligning with the performance levels outlined within Bloom's Taxonomy? Take a second to circle those verbs in the above outcome. What verbs did you highlight? If you selected design and present, you are on the right track. Why is this activity significant within the context of designing an assessment? What purpose does this serve? Identifying the action verb ensures that you create a lesson as well as an aligned assessment at the appropriate performance level.

Let's continue to expand upon this idea. Imagine that you've completed the third-grade science lesson. Students have designed and presented solutions to reducing the impact of natural hazards. You are now ready to craft an assessment item or task for the culminating unit test. What might that item or task entail? How will you ensure that the performance level within the outcome matches the performance level required by the assessment item or task? As an example, your unit assessment might include the below task as a follow-up to the third-grade science lesson.

> **Learning Task: You are a concerned constituent in a community that experiences**
> **heavy flooding during the spring months. Craft a proposal—to present to community**
> **leaders—outlining solutions to reduce the impact of localized flooding. A successful**
> **proposal presents possible solutions and specific information, evidence, proof, or**
> **other supporting details to justify the solutions posed.**

In the above example, identify all action verbs. Next, determine the performance level within Bloom's Taxonomy that each action verb represents. Now, revisit the actual learning outcome. Do the performance levels match? Is there alignment between the assessment task and the outcome for student learning? Why, or why not?

STOP. REFLECT. PLAN. ACT.

Aligning Assessments

Professional Learning Task. In this section, you explored the connections between course objectives, learning outcomes, and assessment design. Take a moment to **stop**, **reflect**, **plan**, and **act**. In your own words, describe the relationship between course objectives, outcomes, and assessments below.

Conclusion

This chapter explored each of the developmental phases, presented as a framework, for mapping the scope and sequence for your class. The process begins with identifying essential knowledge and skills (task, process, or strategy) for the course. This drives the development of objectives and learning outcomes. Next, you organize and sequence objectives and outcomes into logical, coherent units and lessons of study. Lastly, you align assessments with outcomes for student learning.

As we close out this chapter, please remember the critical importance of alignment between objectives, learning outcomes, and assessments. Use the multitude of resources in this chapter to facilitate your work. Also don't forget that your learning outcomes should be specific, measurable, achievable, related, and timely (SMART). In Chapter 7, we'll more deeply explore designing engaging and authentic assessments.

Reflecting for Professional Growth

- What, if anything, did the pandemic teach you about the need for long-term planning and mapping a course's scope and sequence?

- What does "beginning with the end in mind" mean? How do you plan to integrate this design strategy into practice?

- How are course objectives and outcomes for student learning similar? How are they different?

- What's the connection between SMART learning outcomes and the performance levels expected of students? What about SMART learning outcomes and assessment design?

- How do you plan to organize and sequence your units and lessons in the future?

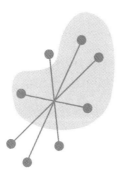

Constructing a Pacing Guide and Establishing Learning Expectations

Outcomes for Professional Learning

In this chapter, we'll discuss:

- Articulating the purpose of a pacing guide

- Establishing learning expectations for students

- Examining pacing guide essentials as opposed to enhancements

- Designing a checklist of pacing guide elements and learning expectations for improved practice

- Evaluating and improving a pacing guide construction template

CONNECTING TO THE ISTE STANDARDS FOR EDUCATORS

The content of this chapter relates to the following indicators:

Learner (2.1.c) Educators stay current with research that supports improved student learning outcomes, including findings from the learning sciences.

Leader (2.2.c) Educators model for colleagues the identification, exploration, evaluation, curation and adoption of new digital resources and tools for learning.

Designer (2.5.b) Educators design authentic learning activities that align with content area standards and use digital tools and resources to maximize active, deep learning.

Designer (2.5.c) Educators explore and apply instructional design principles to create innovative digital learning environments that engage and support learning.

During the pandemic, many students were forced into remote, online, and hybrid learning environments for the first time. Previously, the physical school building and the teacher were central to student learning and monitoring and supporting student progress. As school shifted from learning in a building to learning at home, students and families quickly experienced new levels of flexibility, ownership, and responsibility for learning. From the youngest grades to high school, educators and school leaders quickly realized the importance of student pacing and student pacing guides. Districts, schools, and teachers rapidly began designing and sharing pacing guides with students and families. Parents began appreciating the level of detail and information communicated in pacing guides, as they offered new ways to monitor learning progression and to support student learning. Many parents began reviewing the required course pace and progression and accessing student progress by viewing grades and teacher feedback within a learning management system (LMS). For many families, this was the first time that they knew:

- What their students were learning and when

- What the objectives and learning outcomes being taught were and when

- How students were being assessed and when assessments were due

- How to access student grades to monitor learning progression

- The level of effort and time students were committing to their learning

- How to review teacher feedback for grade improvement purposes

- When and how to access teachers and other resources for additional learner support

- What the learning expectations were for their students

Two things drove this level of parent access, parent knowledge, and parent understanding. First, many schools, districts, and teachers created and shared detailed pacing guides with families. Second, many schools, districts, and teachers leveraged their LMSs as a "hub" for learning and communicating during the pandemic. This provided student—and parent—access to the digital classroom.

As the reimagining of the classroom continues, many students and parents will continue demanding this level of information and access to support their learners. In addition, we anticipate that parents will want pacing guides and the continued ability to monitor student progression via the LMS. In this chapter, we will explore how to design a pacing guide. It's worth noting that creating a student pacing guide is a best practice for any learning environment—in-person, online, or blended.

So what exactly is a pacing guide? In short, a pacing guide presents information about the course of study and defines learner expectations and responsibilities; it's a tool that communicates who, what, when, where, why, and how (Thompson, 2007). Vai and Sosulski (2016) explained that a pacing guide answers many of the following questions for students:

- Who is instructing the course?

- Who is the course designed for?

- What is the course about?

- What is required to be successful in the course?

- What are the expectations for the course?

- What is the grading scale?

- What institutional and course policies should I be familiar with?

- When does the course take place?

- When are synchronous class sessions?

- When are lessons and assessments to be completed/submitted?

- Where are we going in terms of learning?

- Where will learning take place: in-person, online, synchronously, asynchronously?

- Why is the course being taught?

- How do I contact the instructor?

- How do I access learning support and other help?

Take a minute to consider your current pacing guide design practices. What do they communicate about you and your courses? What is currently working well? Are there opportunities for improvement? This chapter will explore how to effectively design a pacing guide, outlining essential elements and other items to enhance this tool.

STOP. REFLECT. PLAN. ACT.

Articulating the Purpose of a Pacing Guide

Professional Learning Task. In this section, we began defining the pacing guide and describing the purpose of this tool. Take a moment to **stop, reflect, plan,** and **act.** In your own words, articulate the primary purpose of a pacing guide.

Examining Pacing Guide Essentials

It can't be overstated that a pacing guide is a learning tool for students. It should integrate all the essential items that will guide students through your course and put them on a pathway to success. The following sections detail the Design Essentials you'll need in your pacing guide, as well as offer recommendations and resources to help you design it.

Design Essential #1: Course Title

Your pacing guide should include the official course title. If you are an elementary, middle, or secondary teacher, you will most likely use the official course code title determined by your state education agency. If you instruct at the college level, use the official title published in your institution's course catalog.

Design Essential #2: Course Description

Early in your pacing guide, include a concise one- or two-paragraph course description. In fact, one of the first items presented in a pacing guide is typically a description of the course (Gannon, 2018). A course description is nothing more than a broad explanation of the significant learning experiences and breadth of instruction. Remember, keep it short and concise.

Design Essential #3: Course Objectives

Course objectives are another vital element of the pacing guide. As you remember from Chapter 3, course objectives, unlike learning outcomes, are broad statements that communicate the focus, direction, and depth of instruction. Because objectives share the wide range of knowledge and skills addressed in the course, they are vital to your guide.

Design Essential #4: Teacher Name and Teacher Contacts

Students need to know who their teacher is and how to contact them. So, in addition to providing your name and position (third-grade teacher, professor of linguistics, teacher's assistant, for example), be sure your pacing guide answers these questions:

- What's your role for this class?

- What is your preferred mode of communication?

- How can students contact you (email address, cell phone number, or other method)?

- Where is your classroom/office (if applicable)?

- When are your office hours, or when can students contact you?

Addressing these questions within the pacing guide will ensure that students know who you are and know how to contact you.

Design Essential #5: Brief Biography

During the pandemic, especially in urban centers, many students and families never got to meet their teachers in-person. To foster connections and relationships, many teachers included a brief biography within pacing guides as well as within the LMS, sharing information about them and their stories. Consider including a biography in your pacing guide that answers the following:

- Who are you?

- What did you study in college and beyond?

- How does your passion intersect with your professional work?

- How does this passion connect to the course?

A biography communicates who you are, how you are uniquely qualified, and why you care, your *why*. So, what's your why? Write it and share it.

Design Essential #6: Teacher Headshot

During the pandemic, many of us didn't get to see or interact with students in person on a daily basis. When students don't see us, we teachers sometimes become abstract figures. New ways of establishing and maintaining the "human connection" were needed. For example, I (James) began including a headshot in the signature line of my email communications with students, parents, teachers, and other school leaders. Why, you might ask? A picture captures your human element that words cannot always express. Showing your face allows students to better relate to you as a person and you as a teacher—so don't be afraid to include a photo of yourself in your pacing guide.

Before you start clicking the shutter button, however, consider the following best practices for taking and selecting that pacing guide or even signature line photo:

- Make sure the picture presents you in a professional demeanor. Use a head-shot or an image that captures you from the shoulders up. Stay away from selfies, as these are normally casual and less formal.

- Be sure to select a high-resolution photo.

- Avoid filters or lenses that distort the original picture.

- Let your personality shine. It isn't a driver's license photo; the goal is to let your warmth and personality transcend. So don't be afraid to smile and slightly tilt your head when presenting your best self.

It's critical to present yourself as a professional in a clear, well-taken picture. A poorly lit, slightly blurry selfie you snapped in haste beside your open refrigerator might send a message, but not the one you intend or that will inspire confidence in your students (or their parents). You can't interact with your students in person every day, so think of ways your photo can help you connect and build relationships. Let your personality shine so that the image invokes a sense of kindness and support.

Design Essential #7: Course Meeting Patterns

In a remote teaching and learning environment, it's vital that everyone involved clearly understands the course's meeting patterns. You can share and even schedule this in the LMS, but you should also communicate the meeting pattern in the pacing guide: When will your class meet? When will learning take place synchronously, and when will learning take place asynchronously? Will synchronous sessions be in-person or stream online? Each of these questions should be considered, planned for, and communicated in your pacing guide. This is true for blended as well as online courses.

Design Essential #8: Unit Titles

The pacing guide should also include the titles of all units of study within your course. In fact, units help frame the overall structure of the pacing guide tool. A unit is similar to a chapter of a book. Chapters provide structure for the book; similarly, units frame and organize the scope and sequence of your blended and even online course. As you remember from Chapter 3, units are broad cohesive segments of instructional content composed of corresponding, sequential lessons. They are presented linearly and communicate the overall direction and pace of learning.

Here's another quick tip for constructing your pacing guide. When creating your unit titles, be sure to follow a standard naming convention. A naming convention is a scheme or pattern for naming items, thereby ensuring consistency throughout your pacing guide and even how you name and present units in the LMS for students. For example, a standard unit naming convention for a United States history course might be:

Unit 2.00 The Revolutionary War

What do you notice? For starters, titling includes *unit* and *2.00*, which together represent the second unit in a sequence of learning units. Additionally, the title captures the broad focus of that unit of learning. As you begin developing unit titles, be sure to take time to craft a naming convention to guide this process for the pacing guide and all other course materials. Your students and their families will appreciate the consistency and organization this brings to your courses.

STOP. REFLECT. PLAN. ACT.
Articulating the Purpose of the Syllabus

Professional Learning Task. In this section, you explored the importance of titling units and the importance of consistent titling. Take a moment to **stop**, **reflect**, **plan**, and **act**. Use the space below to craft a naming convention for unit titles. You will use the naming convention when developing the titles of your units. Remember that a naming convention is a scheme or pattern for naming items.

Design Essential #9: Unit Descriptions

The pacing guide should include a brief description or summary of each unit of study. Typically, you present this information directly under the unit title. As with the course description, a unit description is a broad explanation of the significant learning experiences and breadth of instruction for that particular unit. Unit descriptions are typically limited to a single, concise paragraph within the pacing guide. Be brief and concise when crafting your descriptions.

Design Essential #10: Unit Objectives

The pacing guide should include unit objectives, which are also course objectives. Remember that course objectives are broad statements that communicate the focus, direction, and depth of instruction. Unit objectives are simply those course objectives isolated and taught in that particular unit. This helps focus the teaching and learning experiences specific to that unit instead of the entire course. This also helps communicate to students the focus of instruction for that unit.

Design Essential #11: Lesson Titles

Like unit titles, lesson titles frame and communicate the scope, sequence, and direction of student learning. It's important to remember that a pacing guide is a tool for student learning. Lesson titles provide specific structures that allow students, as well as parents, to monitor the pace and progress of learning based on the teacher's expectations for learning. Hence, the pacing guide should include the titles of all lessons within each unit of study. The unit, within the context of a pacing guide, offers a structure for organizing all lessons within that series of student learning.

A lesson is nothing more than a segment within the larger unit, offering instructional activities, learning materials, and corresponding assessments. Lessons are also organized in a logical, linear way, just like units. Just like unit titling, naming conventions should be used for titling lessons. For instance, here is a lesson title for an American government course constructed using a naming convention aligned with the unit naming convention:

3.03 Ratification of the United States Constitution

As you can see, the naming convention includes the following information:

- Unit number (3)

- Lesson number (.03)

- Lesson title (3.03 Ratification of the United States Constitution)

As you can see, the numbers within the title provide structure and clarity about where the lesson is located within the larger course context. Take a look at the naming convention for a unit. Now, look at the naming convention for a lesson. How do they build upon one another? How do they offer organization and understanding for students and even families that utilize the pacing guide as a learning resource?

STOP. REFLECT. PLAN. ACT.

Titling Lessons

Professional Learning Task. In this segment we explored titling lessons. Take a moment to **stop**, **reflect**, **plan**, and **act**. Use the space below to craft a naming convention for lesson titles. You will use this convention when developing titles for your lessons. Remember that a naming convention is a scheme or pattern for naming items.

Design Essential #12: Learning Outcomes for Lessons

For each lesson, the pacing guide should also present all learning outcomes. Remember, learning outcomes are clear, concise, specific, measurable, achievable, and outcome-based statements about learning. These statements communicate the knowledge or skill (task, process, or strategy) that students should demonstrate upon completing the lesson. Learning outcomes are student-centered and describe what the student can do after engaging in the lesson. Frequently, learning outcomes are expressed as "I can" statements. Think of learning outcomes as achievement goals for students to master. Unlike course and unit objectives, learning outcomes are specific, measurable, and achievable. We've frequently reinforced in this chapter that a pacing guide is a tool for student learning. With that context in mind, why is it critical that learning outcomes are included with the pacing guide?

Design Essential #13: Assessment Titles and Other Information

One of the most important aspects of a pacing guide is assessment information. Listing all assessments (assignments, tests, projects, and so on) and the progression of assessments allows students to self-monitor their learning pace. At the outset, students frequently wonder, "What exactly am I expected to complete and submit to the teacher?" Learners want to know, from day one, exactly what's expected. This allows students to anticipate what's due when and manage their time to ensure proper pacing. Units and lessons also organize and structure how assessments are presented on the pacing guide. Most blended courses, and even online courses, use the same naming convention pattern for lesson and unit titles as well as assessment titles. For instance, here is a lesson title for an American government course:

3.03 Ratification of the United States Constitution

The complementary assignment title for this example is:

3.03 Ratification of the United States Constitution (Essay)

What did you notice? Let's take a second to deconstruct the pattern or structure of the convention below.

- Unit number (3)

- Lesson number (.03)

- Lesson title (3.03 Ratification of the United States Constitution)

- Assessment type (Essay)

You probably noticed that the same, consistent, naming pattern was used for the assessments, except that the assessment type was added. How does this offer organization and consistency for your students?

STOP. REFLECT. PLAN. ACT.

Titling Assessments

Professional Learning Task. In this section, we discussed the importance of including assessment information within the course syllabus. As for unit and lesson titles, we discussed the importance of consistency in how assessments are titled. Take a moment to **stop**, **reflect**, **plan**, and **act**. Use the space below to craft a naming convention for assessment titles. You will use the naming convention when developing the titles of your assessments. Remember that a naming convention is a scheme or pattern for naming items.

Design Essential #14: Due Dates, Deadlines, and Grades Earned

The next Design Essential is due dates, deadlines, and grades earned. Students want to know what's due and when. We all experienced the importance of consolidating and sharing this information with students and families during remote learning in the 2020–2021 school year. Your pacing guide should include all due dates for all assessments (assignments, tests, projects, and so on). In addition, be sure to include any significant deadlines or milestones associated with your course. For instance, students might be completing a personalized project for your class. If there is a deadline to select the topic of study, that should also be included within your pacing guide. Next to each assessment title and assessment due date include a space to enter the student's earned grade. Why? This helps students track and monitor their learning in your course.

Design Essential #15: Guidelines for Course Participation

The pacing guide also needs to outline clear guidelines for course participation. For instance, are synchronous class meetings required? If so, are classes in person or online? What are the dates and times of each session? Is attendance mandatory, and, if so, what are the implications of missing a class session (in other words, what are your attendance expectations)? In addition, during synchronous classes, what are the expectations for your learners? For example, one expectation might entail that "Students must arrive to class on time and be actively engaged the entire time."

Course participation requirements also entail how students interact with the teacher, the course, and the other students. Are there group projects or other collaborative activities? What are the expectations or norms for engaging with other students? What about group discussion boards? What learning, as well as communication expectations, define that type of participation? Does your class have etiquette expectations that students must know and model? When devising your pacing guide, consider and determine all course participation requirements.

Design Essential #16: Academic Competencies

Academic competencies are those behaviors, attitudes, knowledge, and skills that learners need to succeed in your course, so be sure to include them in your pacing guide. When drafting your academic competencies, consider the reoccurring traits modeled by students that typically experience success in your courses. Why were these learners successful? What did these students do differently? Capture that information and transform it into academic competencies. If you are struggling to envision this section of the pacing guide, review the below sample competencies to get you started.

SAMPLE ACADEMIC COMPETENCIES

Students are expected to strive for academic excellence. Successful learners demonstrate academic professionalism, ownership of learning, and superior communication skills. In addition, achieving students attend to detail, read and follow directions, behave ethically and morally, adapt, as well as master time and responsibility. Learners should model the following academic competencies while completing the course:

- The student strives for academic excellence achieving at the highest levels possible.
- The student self-advocates when additional help, support, or other assistance is needed.
- The student exhibits superior communication skills, oral and written.
- The student demonstrates self-motivation and self-discipline.
- The student displays attention to detail in reading and following instructions.

- The student possesses integrity and acts ethically, completing work independently and without unauthorized help.

- The student can adapt and manage competing demands.

- The student takes responsibility for actions and keeps commitments.

- The student masters time management, completing work on time and remaining on pace.

- The student dedicates the time necessary to master the course material successfully.

- The student makes no excuses and is continuously solution-focused.

Now that you have additional context and ideas, it's time to draft the academic competencies for your class and for inclusion in your next pacing guide.

STOP. REFLECT. PLAN. ACT.

Developing Academic Competencies

Professional Learning Task. In this section, we discussed the importance of including academic competencies in your pacing guide. Take a moment to **stop**, **reflect**, **plan**, and **act**. Use the space below to develop a list of academic competencies for your students. Don't forget to integrate your competencies into future course pacing guides.

1.

2.

3.

4.

5.

Design Essential #17: Communication Expectations

The recent pandemic unlocked the door in terms of the modalities and times in which educators instruct and communicate with students and even parents. In blended as well as online classrooms, communication transcended traditional classroom and communication methods. We anticipate that many of these practices will continue, requiring students to become effective communicators as well as model appropriate communication habits. To help them, consider outlining your communication expectations for students in your pacing guide. The following examples and ideas will help you get started.

SAMPLE COMMUNICATION EXPECTATIONS

Students must maintain consistent and regular communication with the teacher. The following expectations are required of all learners enrolled in the course:

- Students are required to have and maintain internet access and a computer for learning purposes.

- Students are required to have access to a working telephone and supply that telephone number to the teacher.

- Students should set up voicemail on their cell phones and check it daily.

- Students should contact the teacher via cell phone only between 8:00 AM and 4:00 PM daily.

- Students must read all teacher posts/announcements.

- Students must respond to teacher communications within twenty-four (24) hours.

- Students are required to submit a Technology HelpDesk Ticket if experiencing a technical challenge.

- Students must participate in discussion boards and group projects, if applicable, offering scholarly, academic-focused contributions.

Any questions or concerns regarding the communication policy should be directed to the teacher of the course.

Which of these expectations apply to your classrooms and students? Which don't? What's missing from the list? Building on these ideas, design student communication expectations for your courses.

STOP. REFLECT. PLAN. ACT.

Designing Communication Expectations

Professional Learning Task. In this section, we reviewed example student communication expectations and described the importance of including this information in your pacing guide. Take a moment to **stop**, **reflect**, **plan**, and **act**. Use the space below to design communication expectations for your next blended class.

1.

2.

3.

4.

5.

Design Essential #18: Discussion Board Expectations

Discussion boards are unique to blended and online environments and should also be addressed in your pacing guide. When leveraged effectively, discussion boards can facilitate engaging student dialog about learning. But engagement doesn't happen by accident; it is an outcome of establishing expectations and norms as well as monitoring those expectations. Ensuring dynamic engagement requires that you actively facilitate discussion boards; it's essential to establish discussion board expectations. Thus, consider integrating your expectations within the pacing guide. The following sample expectations might help spark ideas.

SAMPLE DISCUSSION BOARD EXPECTATIONS

A discussion board is an online forum within the course. Students consider a question or topic and examine varying perspectives by reading, writing, and responding to others (within a discussion thread). A discussion thread is a written dialog on a single question or topic. When participating in discussion boards, students should engage in academically rich conversations. Academically rich conversations are defined as the following:

- Statements backed up with research and references

- Observations connected to the discussion topic

- Reflections on a posting that connect to the student's experiences and knowledge

- Feedback from a personal perspective

- Responses that build on the ideas of others

- Postings that demonstrate an understanding of the lesson's learning outcomes

- Statements that elicit thoughtful reflection and response from other students

- Postings that integrate multiple views and show respect for the ideas of others

- Reflections that dig deeper into the assigned question or topic

Integrating these practices will ensure fruitful discussions about the topic or question posed.

Take a moment to reflect on the discussion board expectations. In a brick-and-mortar class, you typically execute protocols that engage students in the process of learning. How are the above expectations similar to those learning protocols? Also remember to keep your expectations age appropriate. The example expectations were created for high school students. How might you adapt these broad ideas for elementary students?

STOP. REFLECT. PLAN. ACT.

Establishing Discussion Board Expectations

Professional Learning Task. Discussion boards are a common, collaborative feature of the blended classroom. In this section, you discovered the importance of including discussion board expectations in your pacing guide. Take a moment to **stop**, **reflect**, **plan**, and **act**. In the space below, establish student expectations for how learners engage using discussion boards. Use language that is age appropriate for your students. Don't forget to include these expectations in future pacing guides.

1.

2.

3.

4.

5.

6.

7.

8.

9.

10.

Design Essential #19: Technical Requirements and Support

Digital technologies make blended and online learning possible, providing students with flexibility in time, distance, and space for learning—as well as occasional unexpected challenges. To reduce the chances that these technical challenges impede student learning, include your course's technical requirements and support options within your pacing guide.

For instance, which LMS hosts your course or courses? How do students log in? Other examples include software or other tools needed explicitly for your class. In mathematics, it might be pertinent to share an online scientific calculator with students or note that a specific type of calculator must be purchased. For graphic design, learners might need access to Adobe Photoshop or similar software. While technical requirements vary by course, it is essential to include this information.

The pacing guide should also include instructions on how to address technology issues. Who do learners contact to troubleshoot and resolve challenges? Is it you? If so, what's the best means to contact you? If you work for a large institution, your organization probably has a Technology Help Desk. Typically, a Help Desk will serve as a single contact for hardware and software issues, tracking and resolving users' challenges. If your institution doesn't have a Help Desk, then be sure to identify how best to resolve such challenges.

Design Essential #20: Course Timeframe

As educators continue learning and innovating as a result of the pandemic, we anticipate that more districts and schools will experiment with flexible pacing options. For instance, is your course self-paced? If so, are there any time constraints in terms of course completion? Is the course to be completed over a quarter, semester, or even year? The pacing guide should answer these questions, especially if you haven't established specific due dates for your assessments. Your pacing guide should specify the timeframe expectations in which students must complete the course. For a self-paced course, also include the average amount of time in which most students complete the course, and even complete specific units, lessons, and assessments. This will help students plan out their pace in conjunction with the timeframe in which they want to complete your course.

Design Essential #21: Academic Integrity Policy

During the pandemic, many districts and schools quickly become 1:1 with all students having a device for the purpose of learning. For many, this was the first time they had to specifically address academic integrity issues within the blended and online space. Academic integrity is fundamental to a successful learning experience as well as mastery. To reinforce this with your students, your course pacing guide should communicate that plagiarism is strictly prohibited. For this section of the guide, include your institution's academic integrity policy, as well as the consequences associated with violating the policy. If your institution does not have an academic integrity policy, then you will need to craft one for your students. You can use the following sample as a guide in creating yours.

SAMPLE ACADEMIC INTEGRITY POLICY

Plagiarism is defined as copying or using ideas or words from another individual and presenting those ideas or words as the student's own. Plagiarism entails any one of the following:

- Directly copying the work of another person

- Paraphrasing the views of another person without adequately crediting that individual

- Using and failing to credit any work or answers of another individual appropriately

- Recycling previously submitted work

- Using artwork or pictures without citing

Cheating is also strictly prohibited. Cheating is influencing or leading by deceit or artifice as well as practicing fraud or trickery.

If your institution doesn't have an academic integrity policy, you will likely also need to outline the specific consequences for violating the policy. I (James) experienced and addressed many academic issues while serving as principal of a virtual school. In that role, my team and I developed an online academic integrity course. If a student violated our academic integrity policy, I required the student to complete that course before continuing and as a direct consequence of this violation. That said, create progressive policies and remember that the first violation is a teaching opportunity so don't waste it.

STOP. REFLECT. PLAN. ACT.

Crafting an Academic Integrity Policy

Professional Learning Task. In this segment, you examined the importance of including an academic integrity policy within your course's pacing guide. You also evaluated a sample academic integrity policy. Take a moment to **stop**, **reflect**, **plan**, and **act**. If your institution doesn't have an academic integrity policy, use the space below to draft a policy for your blended courses. Also, outline the consequences for violating your policy. Be sure to use student-friendly, positive language when developing your materials.

Academic Integrity Policy:

Academic Integrity Policy Violations:

Design Essential #22: Grading Scale and Practices

The last Design Essential is your grading scale and practices. Students are usually curious about grading, and the pacing guide is a great place to address those questions. So, include detailed information on your grading practices. For example, will grades be presented in point values or percentages? What is required to earn an A, B, C, and so on in your course? If there is an institutional grading scale, include this information as well. Also consider whether you have any specific grading practices, such as a makeup work policy. If so, spell out those practices for students. With the flexibility in terms of time, space, and distance that blended and online learning offers, it's important to communicate whether that flexibility also translates to your grading practices—so make this clear in your pacing guide.

Designing a Pacing Guide Checklist

 As you see, so much goes into artfully developing a pacing guide. We hope our Design Essentials will help you develop, reimagine, or improve your existing pacing guide practices. Integrating our fundamentals will ensure that you communicate all course expectations and place students on a path to success. Moreover, a thorough pacing guide will serve as a useful learning tool and support for your students and families. To support your work, we created the following checklist, which you can download via the QR code. Take a second to review the information and refresh yourself on the essentials we shared.

PACING GUIDE DESIGN ESSENTIALS CHECKLIST

- ○ Course Title
- ○ Course Description
- ○ Course Objectives
- ○ Teacher Name and Contacts
- ○ Brief Professional Biography
- ○ Teacher Headshot
- ○ Course Meeting Patterns
- ○ Unit Titles
- ○ Unit Descriptions
- ○ Unit Objectives
- ○ Lesson Titles
- ○ Learning Outcomes for Lessons
- ○ Assessment Titles and Other Information
- ○ Due Dates, Deadlines, and Grades Earned
- ○ Guidelines for Course Participation
- ○ Academic Competencies

○ Communication Expectations

○ Discussion Board Expectations

○ Technical Requirements and Support

○ Course Timeframe

○ Academic Integrity Policy

○ Grading Scale and Practices

Of the items listed, is there anything that doesn't work for your classroom? If so, cross it out from the list. Is there anything missing that absolutely belongs in your pacing guides? If so, write it in the list. Every teacher and every classroom is different, so every pacing guide will look a little different too. However, there are common items that you will always want to include.

STOP. REFLECT. PLAN. ACT.

Designing Your Pacing Guide Checklist

Professional Learning Task. This section reviews the critical elements or Design Essentials for inclusion in your pacing guide. Take a moment to **stop**, **reflect**, **plan**, and **act**. Based upon your learning, your classroom, your students, and your institution, design a checklist of items for your course pacing guides. Refer to and use your list when creating future pacing guides for your blended classrooms.

1.   6.

2.   7.

3.   8.

4.   9.

5.   10.

Evaluating a Pacing Guide Template

 It's time to bring together everything you've learned in this chapter. The following pacing guide template integrates all the Design Essentials we've discussed and is a great starting point as you begin designing your next pacing guide. (You can scan the QR code to download copies for practice.) Take an opportunity to evaluate the sample template. What changes or enhancements are appropriate to meet the needs of your class, your students, and your institution? As you review the template, also consider how the organization, structure, and style impact your ability to effectively communicate information to your learners. Also, how do these elements impact your students' ability to self-monitor their pace and progression in your classes?

COURSE PACING GUIDE TEMPLATE

Pacing Guide for: *Insert Course Title*

COURSE DESCRIPTION:
Insert Course Description

COURSE OBJECTIVES:
Insert Course Objectives

Headshot	*Insert Headshot*
Teacher Name	*Insert First and Last Name*
Email	*Insert Email*
Cell Phone	*Insert Cell Phone Number*
Office Hours	*Insert Office Hours*
Course Meeting Dates and Times	*Insert Course Meeting Dates and Times*
Professional Biography	*Insert Professional Biography*

Unit 1: *Insert Unit Title*

UNIT 1 DESCRIPTION:
Insert Unit Description

UNIT 1 OBJECTIVES:
Insert Unit Objectives

LESSON TITLE	LEARNING OUTCOMES	ASSESSMENT TITLE	DUE DATE	PERCENTAGE/ POINT VALUE	GRADE EARNED
1.01 *Insert Lesson Title*	*Insert Learning Outcome(s)*	**1.01** *Insert Assessment Title*	*Insert Due Date*	*Insert Percentage/ Point Value*	*Leave Blank for Entry by Student*
1.02 *Insert Lesson Title*	*Insert Learning Outcome(s)*	**1.02** *Insert Assessment Title*	*Insert Due Date*	*Insert Percentage/ Point Value*	*Leave Blank for Entry by Student*
1.03 *Insert Lesson Title*	*Insert Learning Outcome(s)*	**1.03** *Insert Assessment Title*	*Insert Due Date*	*Insert Percentage/ Point Value*	*Leave Blank for Entry by Student*

GUIDELINES FOR COURSE PARTICIPATION:
Insert Guidelines for Course Participation

ACADEMIC COMPETENCIES:
Insert Academic Competencies

COMMUNICATION EXPECTATIONS:
Insert Communication Expectations

DISCUSSION BOARD EXPECTATIONS:
Insert Discussion Board Expectations

TECHNICAL REQUIREMENTS AND SUPPORT:
Insert Technical Requirements and Support

COURSE TIMEFRAME:
Insert Course Timeframe

ACADEMIC INTEGRITY POLICY:
Insert Academic Integrity Policy

GRADING SCALE AND PRACTICES:
Insert Grading Scale and Practices

When integrating the Design Essentials from this chapter, adapt your materials based upon your students' age, knowledge, and skills. This example pacing guide template would be appropriate for high school students, but not a third-grade science class. For instance, a third-grade science course pacing guide would use plain, simple, age-appropriate language. In addition, you might integrate icons or pictures that offer context clues about the words or phrases contained within your pacing guide. Remember that a pacing guide is a learning tool, so make sure it works for your students.

Conclusion

In this chapter, we examined how a pacing guide is more than a list of assignments and due dates. It's both a communication tool and a learning tool. A pacing guide presents the scope, sequence, and depth of learning and the expectations and responsibilities of students. It communicates who, what, when, where, why, and how (Thompson, 2007).

We all experienced the importance of learning protocols and well-developed plans for instruction during the pandemic. Like a learning protocol, the pacing guide consists of well-defined information and actions that help students regulate their learning. It's become instrumental as a tool that supports student progression and a means for parents to monitor their learners' pace. Many students and families have recently used and leveraged pacing guides when completing online and remote learning, and we anticipate that many will expect, if not demand, that this instructional practice continue into the future

 ## Reflecting for Professional Growth

- What's the purpose of a pacing guide? Do your current design practices address the larger goal you've identified?

- Which Design Essentials presented in this chapter are appropriate for inclusion when constructing future pacing guides?

- Where would you place the design of a pacing guide within the larger course design context? Why?

- How does a course pacing guide support instruction? What about student learning?

CHAPTER 5

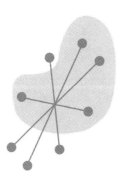

Designing and Delivering Blended Instruction

Outcomes for Professional Learning

In this chapter, we'll discuss:

- Articulating the essentials for designing and delivering blended learning

- Integrating practices to address the social and emotional learning needs of students

- Crafting a framework for providing engaging instruction

- Evaluating and enhancing student discourse practices

- Maximizing comprehension and understanding through feedback and reflection

CONNECTING TO THE ISTE STANDARDS FOR EDUCATORS

The content of this chapter relates to the following indicators:

Collaborator (2.1.c) Educators use collaborative tools to expand students' authentic, real-world learning experiences by engaging virtually with experts, teams and students, locally and globally.

Designer (2.5.a) Educators use technology to create, adapt and personalize learning experiences that foster independent learning and accommodate learner differences and needs.

Designer (2.5.b) Educators design authentic learning activities that align with content area standards and use digital tools and resources to maximize active, deep learning.

Designer (2.5.c) Educators explore and apply instructional design principles to create innovative digital learning environments that engage and support learning.

Facilitator (2.6.d) Educators model and nurture creativity and creative expression to communicate ideas, knowledge or connections.

You'll remember from previous chapters that students in a blended learning environment interact synchronously and asynchronously, at least in part. This means that students use instructional technologies, online resources, and other digital tools to work through a prescribed plan of study, learning, and demonstrating understanding both synchronously and asynchronously and even in-person and remotely. By design, some teachers also allow students to control their learning pace in a blended environment; when students are ready, they complete an assessment to demonstrate mastery. Once a certain level of proficiency is attained, students progress with their learning.

At times blended learning is described in a way that focuses on only the context of education. Because of the technical components, there is hyper focus on instructional technologies instead of teaching and learning. Although technology is essential to delivering blended instruction, it is just one aspect of numerous considerations. To mitigate this issue, many use a *design framework* addressing instructional design considerations specific to blended learning. An instructional design framework supports high-quality instruction and authentic student learning. A framework also ensures that students engage at the highest cognition levels, whether learning synchronously or asynchronously.

In this chapter, we will explore a framework for designing and delivering blended learning. The following design and delivery actions encompass our framework:

- Open with optimism

- Communicate learning outcomes

- Activate prior knowledge

- Build academic vocabulary

- Deliver engaging instruction

- Facilitate student discourse

- Close with optimism

- Extending learning through feedback and reflection

It's important to remember that our framework adapts to both in-person and remote synchronous teaching and learning. That's the magic of our framework—it's universal by design.

Design Essential #1: Open with Optimism

During pandemic, uncertainty and often trauma became part of everyday life for educators and students alike. At the same time, however, there was a renewed sense of community and the social and emotional well-being of others. Many educational leaders and teachers prioritized the social and emotional needs of students above all else. When students don't feel safe and supported, learning becomes more challenging. With that in mind, we must all continue focusing on our students' social and emotional well-being—and maintain this level of attention and focus even as the pandemic subsides.

One way teachers began addressing learners' social and emotional needs was by integrating optimistic welcoming activities during synchronous class sessions (both in person and remotely). The Collaborative for Academic, Social, and Emotional Learning (CASEL) identified welcoming and inclusion activities as one of three signature practices for social and emotional learning integration into classrooms, schools, and workplaces (CASEL, 2019). Welcoming activities set the tone for the day or class and acknowledge that we and our students bring our "whole selves" into those spaces (CASEL, 2019). So before jumping directly into instruction, open the day or the class by welcoming students with optimism. Embed activities, routines, and rituals that welcome inclusion and create optimal conditions for learning.

 Not sure where to begin? That's okay; we've collected and adapted some of CASEL's welcoming activities in the chart that follows, as well as added a few of our own. For additional ideas on opening with optimism, scan the QR code to explore all of CASEL's offerings or go to casel.org.

STRATEGIES FOR OPENING WITH OPTIMISM	
(Adapted from CASEL, 2019)	
STRATEGY	**DESCRIPTION**
Warm and Consistent Greetings	Consistently and warmly greet all students as they enter your classroom or log into your remote, synchronous class sessions.
Scale of Emojis	Create a document including emojis representing a wide range of emotions (six to eight) such as happy, excited, loved, sad, scary, anxious, and so on. As students enter the room, have learners quickly identify the emoji that best represents their current emotions. As students select an emoji, acknowledge their emotion, celebrate the positive and express concern and empathy when appropriate.
	This strategy allows you to understand better the wide range of emotions learners bring with them into class. Leverage this information to fully support students' social and emotional needs both inside and outside the classroom. In a remote environment, before beginning the synchronous class session, have students send you a direct message sharing an emoji that best represents their current emotion.

Continued

STRATEGIES FOR OPENING WITH OPTIMISM	
(Adapted from CASEL, 2019)	
STRATEGY	**DESCRIPTION**
Greeting Frenzy	Structure time for students to engage in a five-minute greeting frenzy. Students should greet everyone in the room by name and share something positive or hopeful during this time. For remote class sessions, break students into smaller group channels to replicate this activity. Again, the goal is to lift the energies of your class by reinforcing positive connections and relationships with one another.
Names and Motions	It's hard for students to feel connected and engaged with one another if they don't even know each other's names, and this is an excellent way for new students to learn them. Have students sit in a circle. Next, ask each student to say their name and make a motion representing something they like doing. Once the student is done, have all students say, "Hi, *[Student's Name]*" and then make the same motion representing what the student likes. Complete the same actions until all students have had a turn as a way to help them get to know one another. This activity is also easily adapted to the remote learning environment.
Class Meetings	Class meetings are another great way to set the tone for the day or class period. Morning meetings allow students and teachers to greet and acknowledge each other daily. They can also be used to celebrate both personal and academic successes. Finally, class meetings allow teachers an opportunity to explain the learning ahead and what to expect. Digital learning technologies also make class meetings easily adaptable to the remote learning environment.

Continued

STRATEGIES FOR OPENING WITH OPTIMISM *(Adapted from CASEL, 2019)*	
STRATEGY	**DESCRIPTION**
Welcoming Routines	Welcoming routines are another great way to set the tone for learning. CASEL (2019) noted that "Welcoming routines include a well-taught system of actions or series of tasks that contribute to an expected rhythm that starts an event." A daily welcoming ritual is basically a list of simple tasks that students are expected to do upon arrival, for example: 1. Pick up the two-page article on climate and environment at the front of the room. 2. Read the article, being sure to circle any unfamiliar words. 3. Look up the definitions of unfamiliar words and capture those definitions in your class journal. Note that welcoming routines must be consistent so learners can become accustomed to systematic, daily routines. Once patterns are recurring, students enter your classroom with a learning mindset and can more quickly focus on the day's learning.

FROM THE FIELD

The Power of Optimistic Welcoming and Closing *by Nicole (Nikki) Healy*

As an educator, I have learned that positive relationships are the most crucial aspect of building a strong learning community. Intertwined with relationship building is a clear and consistent routine. In my classes, I've embedded welcoming students with optimism as well as closing the lesson with optimism.

At the beginning of each synchronous session, I put an agenda in the chat box. "Check-in" is always first on that list. Class begins with an activity that is fun, is bright, and blends with our current learning objective. For example, if we are writing food reviews to demonstrate proficiency in multi-modal writing, I use a This or That prompt. This or That simply prompts learners to choose one of the two options. Students get excited to share their opinions and learn how others feel—especially the teacher! This simple activity sets the tone for a positive and engaging classroom experience where all voices are heard and valued.

Optimism continues even through the conclusion of the lesson. Of course, reminders of upcoming due dates play an essential part, but more importantly, instead of concluding with "Do you have any questions?" I ask "What questions do you have?" This promotes a classroom environment that encourages questions in a safe and welcoming manner. Lastly, but certainly at the center of this "heart-work," I conclude with a tagline of sorts that I have used for years: "You are loved. Be good humans!" I want the final words that students hear in our classroom to be authentic and affirming. I hope that those words carry with them both at school and beyond.

Nicole (Nikki) Healy is an award-winning educator based in Nashville. She served as a classroom teacher for eight years before moving into an Assistant Principal role. She is a devoted advocate for building community and empowering young people through student voice, choice, and culturally sustaining literature. In July 2020, she was selected to receive the Nashville Public Education Foundation's 2020 Inspiring Educator Award.

Design Essential #2: Communicate Learning Outcomes

Now that you've established optimal conditions for learning, it's time to present the outcomes for student learning. Outcomes are most effective when they aren't presented as a to-do list but, instead, in a way that is intrinsically motivating and student-owned. This can occur when learners connect to core concepts communicatively, in ways framed by everyday language. Learning outcomes refer to the content students are studying and include the context of their learning. When creating learning outcomes, you should identify the knowledge or skill (task, process, or strategy) that learners will develop during the lesson. There are several ways to develop learning outcomes, but we recommend using the SMART Learning Outcome method discussed in earlier chapters. SMART outcomes are specific, measurable, achievable, related, and timely.

When presenting your SMART outcomes for learning, the communication must go beyond a written statement visible on the classroom whiteboard or displayed within an online digital platform. You can best support students by connecting academic vocabulary with cognitive terms. The dialogic nature of communicating about concepts helps students to better access new ideas and skills. This means you might create a video to share concrete examples of the learning outcome in action or hold a virtual meeting with students before the lesson to have a more in-depth conversation about the learning.

When developing learning outcomes, it's essential to incorporate the learning context to foster additional clarity and understanding. Consider this example of a learning outcome in a math classroom:

> **I can explain what points on the graph represent when looking at the math problem.**

The student might explain the concept to a student peer or the teacher during a class discussion. The verb *explain* could be replaced with a higher cognitive verb like *demonstrate* if students are using Google Jamboard to graph points with the screen record tool (demonstrating understanding of the concept). In the reimagined classroom, a learning outcome might instead be framed as, "Using screen capture tools, I can confidently demonstrate what points on a graph represent." The example provides the context of the environment as well as the digital learning tool used to achieve the outcome. We created the following framework to help you create and communicate your outcomes for learning.

> **Learning Outcome = Context of Environment + Tool + "I can"
> + Aligned Verb + Conceptual Nouns**

Using the framework, we crafted the following learning outcome.

> **Learning Outcome = Using Google Hangouts, I can collaborate with students
> in other countries to report on a topic with appropriate facts and relevant,
> descriptive details while speaking clearly and at an understandable pace.**

For additional information and ideas on learning outcomes, see Chapter 3, "Mapping the Course Scope and Sequence." For now, remember the importance of communicating outcomes for student learning during your synchronous classes so that students have a clear understanding of the goal and purpose of forthcoming instruction.

Design Essential #3: Activate Prior Knowledge

The next consideration when designing and delivering blended learning is activating the prior knowledge of your students. Learners enter classrooms with varying levels of understanding, experiences, and knowledge. New information is more accessible and likely to be assimilated when presenting it in multiple ways that serve to prime, activate, and provide the needed prerequisite knowledge. Barriers and inequities exist when our students lack the background knowledge necessary to assimilate or use new information. In such instances, we must eliminate inequities by providing multiple entry points for learning.

In the article "Activating Prior Knowledge With English Language Learners," co-author and expert in supporting English learners Larry Ferlazzo described the importance of activating knowledge before introducing complex texts (Ferlazzo & Sypnieski, 2018). He and Katie Hull Sypnieski cited brain research from Carnegie Mellon psychologists, which offered context for why this step is important in building rich understandings and supporting student comprehension. They essentially confirmed that "it's easier to learn something new when we can attach it to something we already know" (Ferlazzo & Sypnieski, 2018), underscoring the importance of activating prior knowledge as well as connecting prior knowledge to new learning.

Dr. Robert Marzano was one of the first educational researchers to cite the value of building background knowledge. Marzano's data revealed that the more prior knowledge learners activate, the more likely students comprehend and retain information (2017). But what about when a learner doesn't have prerequisite knowledge? Without additional support, learning inequalities continue to grow. To address this challenge, you should offer background knowledge and context as well as link prerequisite information to other areas of learning.

Let's take a moment to unpack this concept within delivering instruction in your classroom. Whether designing a third-grade science lesson for a face-to-face lab or streaming a live high school English lesson using digital technologies, begin by activating prior knowledge. You can eliminate inequities by providing multiple entry points for your students. The following strategies will help activate prior knowledge and prime students for the learning ahead.

STRATEGIES FOR ACTIVATING PRIOR KNOWLEDGE		
STRATEGY	**DESCRIPTION**	**DESIGN TOOLS**
Anchoring	Anchor student instruction by linking to and activating relevant prior knowledge (using visual imagery, concept anchoring, concept mastery routines, or other methods).	Embed free stock images into video or online lessons.
Illustrating	Illustrate relationships using advanced organizers or other learning tools (KWL methods, concept maps, and so on).	Create KWL methods and concept maps online so they are editable and shareable.
Pre-Teaching	Pre-teach critical prerequisite concepts by demonstrating or modeling for learners.	Create and upload an instructional video using free online resources, such as WeVideo.
Bridging	Bridge concepts with relevant analogies and metaphors.	Use subtitles and text to bridge concepts or integrate free stock images for metaphorical representations.
Integrating	Integrate explicit cross-curricular connections, such as teaching literacy strategies in a social studies classroom.	Use course design tools that allow for matching as well as explicit feedback on connections.
Guiding	Guide students through an overview of learning objectives, content, or instructional materials.	Create an instructional video or stop motion video to preview materials.

Design Essential #4: Build Academic Vocabulary

Intentionally and consistently introducing and building content-specific vocabulary is the next Design Essential. Vocabulary instruction has a profound impact on student understanding and reading comprehension. Teachers in blended and virtual environments, we cannot forget or abandon the traditional teaching practice of presenting and building vocabulary when designing and delivering instruction to students.

...mic vocabulary ensures that learners have the background knowledge
...ge with the instructional content you're delivering. You must purpose-
...he explicit teaching of academic language vocabulary as a routine
...ing your instruction. Vocabulary instruction is also critical to building
...en mathematical skills. The following chart offers strategies to integrate
...bulary instruction in your classroom.

STRATEGIES FOR BUILDING ACADEMIC VOCABULARY	
TOOLS	**DESCRIPTION**
...es • Google Docs • Google Slides • Video Creator tool	Use cloze passages for steps to build student familiarity with text structures, vocabulary, and comprehension. **Step 1.** Retype a passage and place a blank line in place of strategic words. **Step 2.** Have students read the passage and try to determine from context the terms that might fit in the blanks. **Step 3.** Record a video of you reading the original passage with the words filled in to the class. Discuss whether words students chose that differ from the author's make sense in the context of the passage.

Continued

STRATEGIES FOR BUILDING ACADEMIC VOCABULARY	
STRATEGY & TOOLS	DESCRIPTION

Survival Words
 	
• Google Docs
	This six-step activity uses inquiry to determine how well students understand vocabulary words needed to comprehend a passage, a literary text, or to complete a task successfully.
	
	Step 1. Choose several words that challenge students (academic vocabulary words, tier 2 and tier 3) and are connected to the current unit of study.
	
	Step 2. Have students make a chart with the following six-column headings: Word, A, B, C, D, and Meaning.
	
	Step 3. Ask students to copy each word down in the first column of the chart and check the appropriate A, B, C, or D category for each word.
	
	    A. I know the meaning, and I use the word.
	    B. I know the meaning, but I don't use the word.
	    C. I've seen the word before, but I don't know it.
	    D. I've never seen the word before.
	
	Step 4. Ask students to write the meanings of as many of the words as they know in the meaning column.
	
	Step 5. Break students into groups (or create Google Meet breakout rooms), and ask them to share the words and meanings they are most confident about.
	
	Step 6. Have students create videos or visual representations of words of their choosing.

Continued

STRATEGIES FOR BUILDING ACADEMIC VOCABULARY

STRATEGY & TOOLS	DESCRIPTION
Word Cloud • Wordle, Mentimeter • Google Slides • Google Meet • Google Classroom	This activity stimulates students' thinking about the meaning and relationship of words as they analyze, create, and publish word groupings digitally. **Step 1.** Provide a literary or nonfiction passage to students. **Step 2.** Ask students to paste text into the app and then manipulate the visual display by selecting the color scheme, layout, and font. **Step 3.** Have students paste their word clouds into Google Slides (each student uses their own slide). **Step 4.** Facilitate student discussions on Google Meet or classroom discussion board with such prompts as: • What does the word cloud suggest about the main idea of this passage? • What seem to be the most important words? • How do these words connect to each other?
Cloud-Based Word Wall • Google Docs • Google Drawings (or similar app) • Google Classroom	In this activity, the word wall displays terms used throughout the lesson. Students give meaning to the words on display. Use the following steps to create a cloud-based word wall: **Step 1.** Identify common lesson vocabulary words. **Step 2.** List the words in a Google Docs document or in a post in Google Classroom (or any other LMS discussion board). **Step 3.** As words from the lesson appear during instruction (from an instructional video or from an in-person lesson), have students write the meanings of the words and write an example or draw a picture (Google Drawings or other online drawing tool) in their notes (Google Docs) making sense of the term. When students finish, have them add their work to the whole-class document or the post in Google Classroom. *Tip: Reference the word wall routinely. Have students create their digital word walls to make connections between terms, concepts, and meanings.*

Continued

STRATEGIES FOR BUILDING ACADEMIC VOCABULARY	
STRATEGY & TOOLS	**DESCRIPTION**
KIP Graphic Organizers • Google Docs • Google Drawings	KIP is a graphic organizer that uses a chart to document essential vocabulary for the lesson or unit: key vocabulary (K), information about the vocabulary (I), and a picture (P) drawing of the word. The five steps are: **Step 1.** Create a chart like the one that follows in a Google Docs document. **Step 2.** Have students document the key vocabulary (K) in the table. Don't provide these to students, ask students to choose the key vocabulary based on the passage they're given. Each word will have a chart. **Step 3.** Ask students to write information (I) about the word—their definition for the term, using context clues. **Step 4.** Ask students to draw a picture (P), if appropriate, for the word using Google Drawings or to upload an image. **Step 5.** Have students write or illustrate an example showing the term.

Continued

STRATEGIES FOR BUILDING ACADEMIC VOCABULARY

STRATEGY & TOOLS	DESCRIPTION
Frayer Model • Google Docs • Google Slides	The Frayer Model is a graphic organizer for building academic vocabulary. In a Google Docs document create a two-by-two table (this will become the Frayer Model quadrant). Save the document and share it with students. The below steps describe this model in practice: **Step 1.** Have students write the word they are going to define right above the quadrant graphic organizer. In the paper version, place the word in the middle of the chart. **Step 2.** In the upper-left corner of the two-by-two table, have students write the term's definition in their own words. **Step 3.** In the upper-right corner, have students write any facts or characteristics that they know about the word. **Step 4.** In the lower-left corner, have students write or draw an example of the word. **Step 5.** In the lower-right corner, have students write or draw a non-example of the word. You can use this graphic as a template.

As we've highlighted, when designing instruction for your blended classroom, make sure that you share the academic vocabulary for each lesson and create expectations and experiences where learners will use and integrate the new vocabulary.

STOP. REFLECT. PLAN. ACT.

Designing Strategies that Build Academic Vocabulary

Professional Learning Task. Building academic vocabulary is a design essential for synchronous learning, as presented in this section. Take a moment to **stop**, **reflect**, **plan**, and **act**. In the space below, either:

1.   Improve an existing strategy shared.

2.   Outline an effective strategy in current use.

3.   Research and identify additional strategies.

Don't forget to reference these materials when designing your next synchronous learning event.

#	STRATEGY	DESCRIPTION	TOOL(S)
1.			
2.			
3.			
4.			
5.			

Design Essential #5: Deliver Engaging Instruction

The next Design Essential is delivering engaging instruction—not just instruction, engaging instruction. In Chapter 2, "Planning Essentials for Blended Learning and Beyond," we discussed several blended learning models identified by the Clayton Christensen Institute that have yielded success. While you can leverage any of the models for engaging instruction, in this section, we will look at instructional design through the lens of the Flipped Classroom model.

The Flipped Classroom model is the least disruptive to traditional school structures and is well-suited for school closings due to pandemic or weather-related issues. In this model, learners interact with content via online coursework and teacher-created materials while at home and use in-person opportunities for teacher-guided practice or cooperative learning. In a full-time virtual learning model, the in-person options are replicated using the same online tools used for synchronous learning (Google Meet, Zoom, Google Classroom, and the like).

Flipped learning involves creating or using pre-developed instructional materials, such as instructional videos. In his case study on creating video content for online learning, Stuart Dinmore found that developing instructional videos "increased flexibility" for learning time, place, and pace (Dinmore, 2019), as well as a "sense of personalization and social presence for the learner" (Borup et al. as cited in Dinmore, 2019). Use of videos also offered unlimited opportunities for repetition and revision and resulted in "perceived higher levels of student engagement, promotion of active learning pedagogies, additional language acquisition," and for fully online students, represented "an essential point of contact between teacher and student" as it replaced traditional in-person direct instruction (Dinmore, 2019). No matter what type of resource, with the Flipped Classroom model, initial learning takes place outside of the classroom so that students can engage and work with new knowledge and skills during synchronous class sessions. Achieving this type of structure demands that we create instructional resources that are easily accessible outside of class.

Let's continue exploring how to leverage instructional videos when designing and delivering a flipped classroom. As a default, you might think of recording a traditional thirty-, forty-five-, or even sixty-minute lesson as if you were in a conventional lecture-style classroom. Don't. It won't be the same or as effective as you think. In-person learning includes collaboration, questioning, think-time, and many other components beyond a teacher simply presenting. To ensure the highest levels of student engagement during video lessons, instructional videos should be only six to nine minutes long. Keep them concise, interactive, comprehensive, and impactful. When creating a video, focus on skills and ideas and how you want students to engage with their learning (their learning strategies) throughout the video. Be sure to always include a personal touch, like a greeting or gesture that you and your students share. Or, consider designing a unique opening and closing for each of your videos. Most importantly, don't forget to be dynamic, engaging, and creative. Remember, if your videos don't express excitement about what you're teaching, then students won't experience excitement about their learning. Here's a recap of our favorite design tips for creating instructional videos.

DESIGN TIPS FOR CREATING INSTRUCTIONAL VIDEOS		
Design Tip #1	Keep It Concise	Don't plan the videos as whole replacements for traditional lessons. The final instructional video for a concept should be six to nine minutes long. Keep the video concise, interactive, comprehensive, and impactful.
Design Tip #2	Focus on Knowledge and Skills	Focus on knowledge and skills and how you want students to engage. Think about instructional strategies: questioning, cooperative learning, creation of products, and so on.
Design Tip #3	Personalize It	Always include a personal touch, like a greeting or gesture you and your students share.
Design Tip #4	Keep It Fun	Capitalize on this opportunity for you and your students to learn, grow, and have fun together!

Now, it's time to start planning your first instructional video. How do you pack all your great ideas into six to nine minutes? Use the following framework to get started.

EXAMPLE INSTRUCTIONAL VIDEO FRAMEWORK		
NUMBER OF MINUTES	**VIDEO ELEMENT**	**DESCRIPTION**
0:00–1:00	**Communicating Learning Outcomes**	At the beginning of your video, outline the essential learning for the lesson. Make the context come alive, and remember this is the hook for your lesson.
1:00–3:00	**Activating Prior Knowledge**	Make connections between what students will be learning and what they have already learned. Be sure to incorporate strategies presented in the previous section on activating prior knowledge.
3:00–5:00	**Building Academic Vocabulary**	Highlight new vocabulary in a way that creates meaning, reasoning, and sense-making. Imagery, subtitles, text, and music enhancements will facilitate connections to meaning.

Continued

EXAMPLE INSTRUCTIONAL VIDEO FRAMEWORK		
NUMBER OF MINUTES	**VIDEO ELEMENT**	**DESCRIPTION**
5:00–7:00	**Questioning and Modeling**	Next, engage in questioning and modeling. Questions and think-alouds can be executed using such stems as: • "I know this because..." • "My solution path looks like this..." • "I agree with this approach because..." Be sure to build in video stops where learners can pause and reflect on your questions. If you are sharing new knowledge or modeling new skills, be sure to embed stopping points that enable students to practice the new concept or skill.
7:00–9:00	**Creating Closure and Assessing**	Finally, create closure and assess learning. Closure strategies are presented in greater detail later in the chapter. At the end of the video, share with students how you will evaluate their learning. Also, communicate any next steps. For example, will students now begin a collaborative project to demonstrate their new knowledge and skills? Or, will students create a video explaining their learning? Whatever the subsequent steps, be sure to share that with your students.

You can also use the following prompts as a guide and scaffold as you create your own videos.

EXAMPLE PROMPTS FOR INSTRUCTIONAL VIDEOS

1. I think this about the story so far...

2. This story reminds me of...

3. I need more information about...

4. The author is writing about this because...

5. I reread that part because...

6. I was confused by...

7. I think the most interesting part is...because...

8. That is interesting because...

9. I wonder why...

10. I just thought of...

After you've planned and produced your instructional video, it's showtime for students. Share your creations with students via email, within the LMS, or other platforms that offer this functionality.

STOP. REFLECT. PLAN. ACT.

Instructional Video Framework

Professional Learning Task. In this section, you reviewed a sample framework for creating instructional videos. Our framework is only one of many structures for creating videos. Take a moment to **stop**, **reflect**, **plan**, and **act**. In the space below, design a framework that will guide how you execute instructional videos. You can research other structures integrating those items that work best for you and your learners. Alternatively, you can use the framework we've presented and adapt or improve it for your purposes.

NUMBER OF MINUTES	VIDEO ELEMENT	DESCRIPTION

FROM THE FIELD

Instructional Videos

Educators at Tuggerah Public School, a primary school in Australia, introduced instructional videos to help students and parents cope with learning during the pandemic. Since then, videos have become embedded in nearly every aspect of life at this school, from classroom teaching and homework to school assemblies to staff and community communication. Videos dealing with all key learning areas—from math and spelling to art, music, and cooking—have been produced and uploaded to the school's website. Students have access to videos at any time to practice what they have learned or reflect on new concepts. Originally made to help children and parents at home, the videos are now being used in the classroom for differentiated learning and everyday teaching practice. For example, when a teacher is working with one group of students in class, another group can work independently with the help of an instructional video. The videos have inspired students to use their imaginations, teaching them how to shoot and edit video, and how to create storyboards. With the return to face-to-face teaching at school, students can still access videos from home to learn languages, receive art or music instruction, or to improve their literacy and math learning.

Design Essential #6: Facilitate Student Discourse

Facilitating student discourse involves supporting students in talking through and processing their knowledge or skills. At the heart of discourse is communication, as it builds critical digital age skills like collaboration and teamwork. Thus, effective discourse can serve as a powerful instructional vehicle for creative thinking and learning. This activity supports understanding, connection, and language acquisition; and by increasing student interaction, it also fosters active as opposed to passive learning. Let's examine student discourse as a crucial element of an engaging blended learning experience.

STOP. REFLECT. PLAN. ACT.

Student Discourse Self-Assessment

Professional Learning Task. Before proceeding with facilitating student discourse in your blended classroom, assess the extent of your current student discourse practice. Take a moment to **stop**, **reflect**, **plan**, and **act**. In the space below, review each of the self-assessment questions and select how frequently it occurs: Never, Sometimes, or Always.

Never	Some-times	Always	SELF-ASSESSMENT QUESTIONS
○	○	○	Do I avoid asking, "Do you have any questions?"
○	○	○	Do my questions promote total student involvement?
○	○	○	Do I allow students to use Think-Pair-Share before responding to questions?
○	○	○	Do I redirect specific questions and responses back to the entire class?
○	○	○	Do I create a classroom environment that makes it safe for students to be wrong and even celebrate errors as a learning opportunity?
○	○	○	Do I pause or give at least three to five seconds of wait time before calling on a student?
○	○	○	Do I allow a student to respond to another student's responses before I comment myself?
○	○	○	Does my questioning give me meaningful input about the students' understanding of the concepts I'm teaching?
○	○	○	When there are only a few hands raised to respond to a question, do I provide alternative ways to respond to get more students to participate?
○	○	○	When only one student can answer a question, do I use this input to help others engage?
○	○	○	Do I allow students to discuss ideas with their partners before asking a particular student to share ideas with the entire class?

Balanced student discourse can occur as a whole or a small group, between teacher and student, between student and student, or between students and students. In thriving, learner-centered classrooms, discourse is intrinsically motivated and naturally initiated by students. You can foster the conditions for discourse by modeling effective questioning, thereby setting students up for success. Don't forget to model when recording instructional videos or crafting discussion board prompts. Always consider how you're using questioning to promote student discourse in your classroom.

Is student discourse a staple in your class practice, or are you just beginning to increase engagement by integrating this strategy? Take a moment to reflect on the extent of this practice in your classes.

Take a moment to review your answers. What do the results indicate about your practice? Are you always, sometimes, or never engaging students in discourse? If there are growth opportunities, we can help get you started. If you are just getting started with student discourse, prompting is an easy way to grow this learning activity in your classroom. Consider incorporating the following prompts into your classroom as you are reinforcing lesson concepts and ideas:

- Do you agree or disagree with what was discussed and why?

- Who can add on to what was said?

- What is another way to say what was said?

- Can you repeat what was just said?

- Can you say that in your words?

- Will this strategy always work, and why or why not?

Student sentence starters also support whole-group discourse. Here are some example sentence starters to get students talking and engaging with concepts and ideas from the lesson:

- I agree with...because...

- I respectfully disagree with...because...

- I understand what you're saying, but I have a different idea about...

- Wait, I'm not sure I understand. Can you please repeat...

- So, I hear you saying...

- How did you arrive at...

Consistent, effective student discourse can foster higher-level cognitive thinking in your learners, providing them with opportunities to share, compare, contrast, reflect, revise, and refine ideas. This strategy allows students to process their thoughts before sharing with another student, helping them organize their thinking creatively and in meaningful ways after discussing with others. This is why student discourse is an absolute must for not only blended learning, but all learning environments.

STOP. REFLECT. PLAN. ACT.

Crafting Sentence Starters for Student Discourse

Professional Learning Task. To effectively execute new strategies, you must have a plan. In this section, we discussed the importance of student discourse and examined sentence starters that help facilitate discourse in classrooms. Take a moment to **stop**, **reflect**, **plan**, and **act**. In the space below, identify, enhance, or craft sentence starters that demand student conversation and higher thinking levels. Don't forget to post or reference this information as you develop discourse in your blended classes.

Sentence Starters:

1.   6.

2.   7.

3.   8.

4.   9.

5.   10.

Design Essential #7: Close with Optimism

Lesson closure doesn't happen just by telling students that the lesson is over and it's time to review the lesson outcomes. It is so much more than a quick formative check, exit ticket, thumbs up/down, or question prompt to journal (although these can be useful tools, as you'll learn in Chapter 8, "Maximizing Academic Feedback"). Lesson closure invites and establishes finality. It's an intentional activity that requires learners to reflect on their understandings of new concepts in self-directed ways while also looking forward on a positive note. Lesson closure provides a bridge between the learning that occurs now and the teaching that will happen in the future.

One of our favorite strategies is student-led closure, which can result in deeper learning for students and deeper teacher insight into students' understanding of essential concepts and skills. With this approach, it's important to consider how you can provide students with options to personalize their closure activity so that it's relevant, authentic, and meaningful. When designing lessons, make sure to create closure opportunities where students circle back to the what, the why, and the how of their learning—ending on a positive. This allows students to synthesize their knowledge into broader contexts and look forward on an optimistic note. Also consider routines and practices that engage students in leading lesson closures as opposed to closure always being teacher-led.

When asking students to discuss concepts as part of this process, we all must go further than telling learners to "share your answer with a shoulder partner." A blended classroom requires that teachers use a modified and more appropriate strategy. Conversations should build on a prompt that is aligned to learning objectives, engaging (use technology to respond), instructionally challenging, highly cognitive, and conducive to multiple entry points and solution pathways. Prompts to initiate discourse should be posed in ways that invite wonder, speculation, and exploration by students.

For instance, try turning an exit ticket prompt into an engaging closure activity by having students create a video reflection. In this learning experience, students engage by questioning the reasoning of their peers. Another strategy that works is Think-Pair-on-Air. Instead of students sharing their conclusions and thinking during class, they create a video to share on the class YouTube channel. WeVideo is another useful tool in creating these video-based closure experiences.

Based on the closure prompt, teachers should encourage students to talk about how or why they did what they did or about what they believe. Most importantly, the class-room culture must support curiosity and sense-making, which is demonstrated in the questions students ask in their reflection videos and to one another. Once videos are published and shared with the class, students must build on each other's thinking and generate arguments based on their views. Teachers can ask for justification and encourage students to question and extend their thinking, even after the video creation process is over. The next time you design a closure activity for students, try a video-based activity for a rigorous, engaging, and meaningful student experience. Explore the following chart for strategies to create closure in your blended classroom.

STRATEGIES FOR CREATING CLOSURE	
STRATEGY	**DESCRIPTION**
On Your Way Out	On Your Way Out is a great closure activity for a thirty- to ninety-second gap before student dismissal. For this activity, have learners discuss academic vocabulary—defining terms as they exit the classroom or Google Meet/Zoom.
Thumbs Up/ Thumbs Down/ Emoticons	For Thumbs Up/Thumbs Down/Emoticons, pose questions that students can answer with a thumbs up, thumbs down, or choice of emoticon. To engage students in higher-order thinking, have them explain the rationale for their decisions. Zoom and Google Meet allow students to comment with emoticons.
What Am I?	For What Am I? have students construct clues or riddles about the lesson's key terms in a Google Docs document. Then, have students quiz one another sharing the document with each other.
Jeopardy	In Jeopardy, the teacher provides an answer. Students then create and pose a question. This activity works best with dry erase boards. An online quiz platform like Kahoot! helps teachers create interactive *Jeopardy*-style games.
Be the Teacher	In Be the Teacher, learners are challenged to develop and present three key ideas everyone should have learned during the lesson.
I Care Why?	"I care why?" is a great question. In this activity, students explain the relevance of the concept to their lives or how they might use it in their daily lives. Students can create one-minute videos of their why.

Continued

STRATEGIES FOR CREATING CLOSURE	
STRATEGY	**DESCRIPTION**
Daily Dozen Sentence Stems	For the Daily Dozen activity, students choose two stems about the day's lesson from a generic list. The following will get you started: • The thing that made the most sense to me today was... • One thing that I don't understand is... • When someone asks me what I did in class today, I can say... • One thing I would like more information about is... • I need more examples of... • I enjoyed... • The most important concept that we discussed today was... • Today's class would have been better if we had... • I was confused by... • The thing we did in class today that best fit my learning style was... • The one thing the teacher did today that best fit my learning style was... • The one thing the teacher did today that did not work well for me was... • This point was obvious... • One thing that squares with stuff I already know is... • An idea that is still going around in my head is... Students can post their responses in an online discussion post, create a video, or email the teacher.
Sell It	Sell the idea of the lesson in Sell It. For this activity, students create a jingle that explains and "sells" the lesson's primary purpose. WeVideo contains royalty-free music that students can use for their jingle.
Key Words	Select five critical words used in the lesson for the Key Words activity. Ask learners to identify five words, record them in a Google Docs document, and share it with you. Compare your keywords to the students' keywords to determine whether students grasp the lesson's key understandings.
Whip Around	In Whip Around, students quickly share one thing they learned during the lesson. You can have learners self-select by calling on each other in a Google Meet. Or when you're in grid view, ask students to choose someone in a specified quadrant.

Continued

STRATEGIES FOR CREATING CLOSURE	
STRATEGY	**DESCRIPTION**
3-2-1	**3-2-1** entails students sharing three things they learned, two things they have a question about, and one thing students want the teacher to know. These can be captured on paper, Post-its Notes, index cards, collaborative documents, or a student-created video.
Fishbowl	The Fishbowl activity has a student write one question they have about the topic of the current lesson. The question can be something the learner knows the answer to or something a student wants an answer to. Next, have students form an inner and outer circle. Students then share a question with persons directly in front of them, seeing if other students know the answer. Continue this activity by having students rotate to new partners. This can be done in Google Meet or Zoom by identifying those who will be muted and those who will keep their microphone on.
Three Ws	Three Ws involves learners either writing or discussing the following prompts: • What did I learn today? • So what? • Now what?
Quick Doodles Doodle	In Quick Doodles Doodle students draw two or three concepts presented in the lesson. To expand this activity, students might present and discuss their creations. Students can create online drawings to share with their teacher and fellow students using Google Jamboard.
Postcard	For the Postcard activity, learners are asked to use a platform like Canva to create a postcard explaining the day's lesson.
It Fits Where?	In the It Fits Where? closing activity, students create a timeline or storyboard of the concepts taught (sequencing the concepts or explaining connections to previous learning). A student-created video is an engaging way of representing the timeline.
Where Are We Going?	Where Are We Going? challenges students to predict the focus of the next lesson. Be sure to refer to the predictions, during the next lesson, as either an opener or closure.

Continued

STRATEGIES FOR CREATING CLOSURE	
STRATEGY	**DESCRIPTION**
Commercial	The Commercial activity entails students writing a one- to two-minute commercial that answers the prompt, "What happened in class today? Then the students create a video from their written script.
Four Box Synectics	Four Box Synectics promotes fluid and creative thinking by comparing two things that would not usually be compared. The activity involves the following steps: **Step 1**. Prepare a chart of the Four Box Synectics organizer in Google Docs. **Step 2.** Put students into small groups of three or four students each. **Step 3.** Next, ask for four items in an assigned category, such as commonly found household objects, animals, things found in a forest, recreational activities, or foods. Place one item in each of the four boxes. **Step 4.** Reveal the sentence "A _____ is like a _____ because..." and allow groups three minutes to brainstorm sentences using each of the four items at least once. Students should try to complete as many sentences as they can in the time allotted. **Step 5.** After three minutes, stop. The final step is for each group to choose the two sentences they like the best and share them with the rest of the class. An example Four Box Synectics chart is shown below.

A _____ is like a _____ because...

Continued

STRATEGIES FOR CREATING CLOSURE	
STRATEGY	DESCRIPTION
Numbered Heads Together	For Numbered Heads Together, organize and number students sequentially in groups of no more than five. Groups then create a list of three to five things learned during the lesson. Next, the teacher calls one number from each group to share with the class something they learned. Students can be grouped into Google Meet or Zoom breakouts.
Exit Slip	For the Exit Slip activity, provide students with a paper slip, discussion board prompt, or prompt embedded into a teacher-created instructional video with a question or questions to be answered in a designated time.
Think-Pair-Share	In Think-Pair-Share, students consider a question, prompt, or topic taking individual time to consider what's been posed. After an appropriate amount of thinking time, students pair with another student or small group to share their perspectives and ideas. Finally, pairs or groups of students share the most profound views and thoughts during a whole-class discussion.

Design Essential #8: Extending Learning Through Feedback and Reflection

The final Design Essential for the blended classroom is extending learning through feedback and reflection. In Chapter 8, "Maximizing Academic Feedback," we discuss how to leverage feedback as a tool to support student learning. For now, let's develop a general understanding of what feedback is and its purposes. In *Challenging Learning Through Feedback*, James and Jill Nottingham (2017) described academic feedback as providing information about the knowledge, the task, the process, or the student's strategy.

Feedback and reflection allow students to close the gap between where they want to be and where they are now. Academic feedback supports student thinking in the following ways:

- Understanding the learning outcome

- Knowing where the student is in relation to the learning outcome

- Realizing what the learner needs to do to bridge the gap between the current position and the learning target (Nottingham & Nottingham, 2017).

In short, quality feedback helps learners answer the below crucial questions (Nottingham & Nottingham, 2017):

- What am I trying to achieve?

- How much progress have I made so far?

- What should I do next?

Feedback also addresses any misconceptions or misunderstandings that students have about their learning.

As you can tell, praise is not the same as academic feedback. Feedback is actionable, improving student comprehension and understanding. Providing high-quality feedback is one of the most critical roles of a teacher in a blended environment. Academic feedback should be timely, consistent, and differentiated; it can be shared both synchronously and asynchronously throughout the duration of the course. We discuss this in more detail in Chapter 8.

Conclusion

When reading this chapter, did you notice any similarities in teaching practice, whether in-person, blended, or online? You probably did. You likely identified intersections regardless of the method of instructional delivery, and that's because many effective instructional practices transcend the walls of a traditional classroom. No matter which learning environment you're teaching in, don't throw out best practices that were effective during in-person instruction. The beauty of blended learning is the ability to leverage technology and learning theory in creative ways to meet students' unique needs.

As you begin to incorporate the chapter's eight Design Essentials, we encourage you to think about how each aspect is enhancing instructional practice and student learning. When implementing the instructional framework presented, remember that your focus is not to use as many technology tools as possible. Instead, the focus is to make learning accessible, engaging, and meaningful for all your students.

Reflecting for Professional Growth

- How are you addressing the social and emotional needs of students in your classes?

- What's the connection between communicating outcomes and student learning? Why is it important?

- How do you currently activate prior learning in your classes? Which strategies from this chapter do you plan to integrate into your current instructional practices?

- Why should you integrate content-specific vocabulary into blended instruction?

- What are additional ways of delivering blended instructional lessons to students?

- How might Bloom's Taxonomy inform planning for student discourse?

- Why is closing with optimism and reflection important?

- How can you extend student learning by leveraging teacher feedback and student reflection?

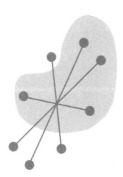

Designing and Delivering Virtual Instruction

Outcomes for Professional Learning

In this chapter, we'll discuss:

- Communicating the essentials for designing and delivering virtual learning within an asynchronous construct

- Developing a virtual lesson framework that presents the outcomes for student learning

- Integrating design practices that activate the prior knowledge of students

- Embedding academic vocabulary instruction within virtual lessons

- Deploying self-assessment opportunities within virtual lessons and engaging students with automated feedback

- Creating lesson closure and previewing the parallel assessment

CONNECTING TO THE ISTE STANDARDS FOR EDUCATORS

The content of this chapter relates to the following indicators:

Learner (2.1.a) Educators set professional learning goals to explore and apply pedagogical approaches made possible by technology and reflect on their effectiveness.

Learner (2.1.b) Educators pursue professional interests by creating and actively participating in local and global learning networks.

Leader (2.2.a) Educators shape, advance and accelerate a shared vision for empowered learning with technology by engaging with education stakeholders.

Collaborator (2.4.a) Educators dedicate planning time to collaborate with colleagues to create authentic learning experiences that leverage technology.

The closing of schools and the shift to new ways of instructing students during the COVID-19 pandemic resulted in a disruption of learning for many. To begin combating these issues, we anticipate that many districts and schools will use diagnostic tools to assess current levels of student understanding. This critical information will provide actionable data to differentiate instruction for students as schools move forward. Some districts and schools have even begun acquiring and using software-based intervention programs to begin addressing distinct learning needs.

As a teacher, you must consider how to differentiate instruction within your classroom to manage many of these challenges. One strategy to personalize learning is developing on-demand asynchronous, virtual lessons that are accessible within a learning management system (LMS). By creating virtual lessons and strategically assigning those lessons based upon diagnostic data, you can individualize learning and address some of the issues associated with learning disruption during the pandemic. This chapter focuses on essential design strategies for developing asynchronous lessons deployed on demand and virtually in the classroom.

Engaging, asynchronous, virtual lessons are a lot like good textbooks. A good textbook captivates the reader with exciting and dynamic content. Textbooks are logically sequenced, offering a clear beginning, middle, and end. One chapter naturally flows into the next with explicit attention to transitions and connections to prior learning. Textbooks also introduce learning outcomes at the beginning of each chapter and present content-specific vocabulary and definitions for that unit of study. A well-designed text also chunks information into easily digestible segments while using examples, pictures, stories, and other strategies to reinforce understanding. Moreover, textbooks frequently provide learners opportunities to self-assess knowledge and performance, as well as direct students to additional resources for support. These same features are also your best foundation for designing asynchronous virtual lessons within an LMS.

Virtual lessons should be presented consistently throughout your course with the basic skeleton of each lesson following the same prescriptive pattern. While structures may vary, we suggest the following design framework for creating and sequencing asynchronous virtual lessons:

- Introduce the lesson and communicate the learning outcomes

- Activate prior knowledge

- Build academic vocabulary

- Deliver engaging instruction

- Provide opportunities to self-assess and automated feedback for students

- Create closure and preview the assessment

To help you better understand each section of the framework, the following sections focus on each area individually.

Design Essential #1: Introduce the Lesson and Communicate the Learning Outcomes

All lessons begin with an introduction of some sort. Think of the introduction as a student's roadmap to the entire lesson. Because you are designing and delivering instruction asynchronously and virtually, the roadmap becomes critical for students because you will not be readily available to answer their questions. The introduction launches the lesson, presents lesson topics and subtopics, shares outcomes for student learning, previews related activities and assessments, and offers closure to the opening. When crafting the introduction to your lesson, be sure to:

- Launch the lesson

- Present the topic

- Preview subtopics

- Share learning outcomes

- Preview activities and assessments

- Conclude the introduction

 The following chart unpacks each of these essential items, offering a framework for opening your lesson and presenting learning outcomes. To download a copy, scan the QR code.

A FRAMEWORK FOR INTRODUCING A LESSON AND COMMUNICATING THE LEARNING OUTCOMES	
ELEMENT	**DESCRIPTION**
Launching the Lesson	Launch the lesson with a catchy opening that grabs or piques the interest of your students. Alternatively, introduce your virtual lesson using a real-world example of how subsequent learning connects to the world around them. You can also launch by offering compelling questions or activities that forecast the lesson's topic and subtopics. You might choose to begin with a story that connects to the focus of learning. However you decide to open, be sure the launch captures students' imagination and invites learning engagement.
Presenting the Topic	Next, present the lesson's topic or focus, so students know what the lesson is about and where they are going. Lesson topics are the broad focus or subject of learning. Topics encompass all subtopics as well as the learning outcomes for the lesson.

Continued

A FRAMEWORK FOR INTRODUCING A LESSON AND COMMUNICATING THE LEARNING OUTCOMES	
ELEMENT	**DESCRIPTION**
Previewing Subtopics	After presenting the topic of the lesson, it's equally important to preview the subtopics. Subtopics are segments that together comprise the broader subject of study (the topic). Subtopics are also grounded in the lesson's learning outcomes. When sharing subtopics in the introduction, address the subtopics in the same order presented in the virtual lesson. This reinforces organization, structure, and flow for students.
Sharing Learning Outcomes	When introducing a lesson, it's also important to share all learning outcomes. In previous chapters, we highlighted the SMART (specific, measurable, achievable, related, timely) Learning Outcome method for developing your outcomes for student learning. Don't forget that learning outcomes measure knowledge (information) or skill (task, process, or strategy). Learning outcomes should be student-centered, describing what the learner can do after completing the virtual lesson. Frequently, learning outcomes are expressed as "I can" statements. A helpful framework to use is: Learning Outcome = Context of Environment + Tool + "I can" + Aligned Verb + Conceptual Nouns Here's an example crafted using the framework: Learning Outcome = Using Google Hangouts, I can collaborate with students in other countries to report on a topic with appropriate facts and relevant, descriptive details while speaking clearly and at an understandable pace. Don't forget that learning outcomes drive lesson content development and the corresponding assessment, so take time to get them right.
Previewing Activities and Assessments	Be sure to preview information about lesson activities and assessments. Are "checks for understanding" found throughout the lesson? If so, highlight that information and the importance of completing each activity. Also, share information about the lesson's corresponding assessment. Is it a quiz? A project? A group activity? Use the introduction as an opportunity to share what students should anticipate when completing the lesson, materials, and assessment.
Concluding the Introduction	Finally, conclude your lesson's introduction. You might bring closure with a pondering question or compelling idea that reinforces the focus of the lesson. You might also choose to summarize information about the lesson's focus. Or, a conclusion might directly connect back to the opening of your introductory section. Whatever direction you go, be sure to bring closure to this segment of the lesson.

For consistent organization, structure, and flow, the introduction should always be presented first. Also, you and your students might find it beneficial to organize all openings similarly. But what exactly does that mean? Consider using or adapting the following template for organizing and presenting the written portion of a lesson introduction. (Scan the QR code for a downloadable version.)

VIRTUAL LESSON INTRODUCTION SECTION TEMPLATE

Lesson 1.01 *Insert Lesson Title*

LESSON LAUNCH:
Insert the Lesson's Launch

TOPICS AND SUBTOPICS:
Insert Information Regarding the Lesson's Topics and Subtopics

Your learning outcomes for this lesson include the following:

- I can: *Insert Learning Outcome*

- I can: *Insert Learning Outcome*

- I can: *Insert Learning Outcome*

Begin your studies by reviewing all the lesson materials. *[Insert Lesson Activities]* When you have completed the lesson and all related activities, complete Assessment 1.01 *[Insert Assessment Type]*. Assessments are found in the *[Insert Location Information]* section of the course.

Be sure to keep track of your learning by taking notes on the concepts presented in the course. Place your notes together in a safe place. Taking notes will help you prepare for course assessments, activities, and your final exam. If you have any questions regarding this lesson, be sure to contact the course instructor.

CONCLUSION:
Insert Conclusion

Utilizing the tools, structures, and examples presented ensures your lesson introductions are consistent, organized, and logical. Why is this level of organization and consistency so important? Consider the effect of standardizing how you develop and present introductions. What, if any, result does this have on student learning? How do you know?

STOP. REFLECT. PLAN. ACT.

Designing a Virtual Lesson Introduction Section Template

Professional Learning Task. Now that you've learned about designing the introduction to a virtual lesson, take a moment to **stop**, **reflect**, **plan**, and **act**. Remember that the introduction launches the lesson, presents lesson topics and subtopics, shares outcomes for student learning, previews related activities and assessments, and offers closure to the opening. Now, review the **Virtual Lesson Introduction Section Template** and other materials in this section. Using the space below, adapt or develop a lesson introduction template that meets your student-specific needs, course-specific needs, and institution-specific needs. As you begin creating virtual lessons, be sure to revisit this design template and follow the structures you've built.

Design Essential #2: Activate Prior Knowledge

Students enter the classroom with varying backgrounds, experiences, and knowledge levels. This prior knowledge—what students already know or have experienced—offers meaning, context, and links to the new learning students are about to experience. Therefore, to increase student comprehension and understanding, it's vital to build upon this foundation—to activate that knowledge. This level of conditioning prepares students for the learning ahead and supports ultimate connections and mastery of the lesson's outcomes.

Connecting prior learning to current learning is a powerful instructional strategy and should be addressed after the introduction when designing your virtual lessons. There is a direct relationship between the connections made to prior knowledge and students' acquisition of new knowledge and skills. As you begin leveraging this strategy, explore the following graphic for additional design ideas.

STRATEGIES FOR ACTIVATING PRIOR KNOWLEDGE		
STRATEGY	DESCRIPTION	DESIGN IDEAS
Anchoring	Anchor student instruction by linking to and activating relevant prior knowledge. Using visual imagery, concept anchoring, or concept mastery routines, for example.	Embed free stock images into your video or online lesson.
Illustrating	Illustrate relationships using advanced organizers or other learning tools, such as KWL methods and concept maps.	You can create editable and sharable KWL methods and concept maps online.
Pre-teaching	Pre-teach critical prerequisite concepts by demonstrating or modeling for learners.	Create and upload an instructional video using free online resources, such as WeVideo.
Bridging	Bridge concepts with relevant analogies and metaphors.	Use subtitles and text to bridge concepts or integrate free stock images for metaphorical representations.
Integrating	Integrate explicit cross-curricular connections. For example, you could easily teach literacy strategies in a social studies classroom.	Use course design tools that allow for matching as well as explicit feedback on connections.
Guiding	Guide students through an overview of learning objectives, content, or instructional materials.	Create an instructional video or stop motion video to preview materials.

Consider the effect of integrating the above strategies into lesson design. What is the impact on instruction? What about student learning?

Design Essential #3: Build Academic Vocabulary

Have you ever visited a foreign country and didn't speak the native language? Over your stay, you probably learned several critical words that helped you navigate the new world around you. As you started acquiring the new language, you likely leaned on your beginning vocabulary to learn new words and their meanings. The same is true in the classroom: Students need support with new or unfamiliar terminology. It's essential to highlight and deconstruct unknown vocabulary to help students develop the meaning of these new terms. As students are reading or experiencing further information, this offers context for knowledge and skill acquisition.

The next section of your virtual lesson should address and build your students' vocabulary, specifically *academic vocabulary*. Academic vocabulary refers to the unique or uncommon words students encounter while engaging in the learning process. Academic vocabulary is specific to your content or discipline. These terms are less frequent in everyday conversations and might be altogether new to your students.

 For these reasons, the third section of your virtual lesson presents the academic vocabulary to learners. Academic vocabulary is critical for students that don't have the knowledge or context to comprehend the lesson without added support. Presenting vocabulary within each lesson builds context that is essential for understanding. Thus, it is best to explicitly teach academic vocabulary in each virtual lesson you create. The following graphic presents a template for introducing and highlighting the vocabulary for an asynchronous virtual lesson. (Scan the QR code for a downloadable version.)

VIRTUAL LESSON ACADEMIC VOCABULARY SECTION TEMPLATE

It is essential to become familiar with the critical academic vocabulary presented in the lesson. Academic vocabulary refers to unique or uncommon words that you will likely encounter when reviewing lesson materials. Below you will find each vocabulary word for this lesson and an explanation of each concept.

- *[Insert Vocabulary Word]: [Insert Definition]*

- *[Insert Vocabulary Word]: [Insert Definition]*

- *[Insert Vocabulary Word]: [Insert Definition]*

Reviewing and understanding the lesson's vocabulary supports your learning and mastery of the lesson's learning outcomes. It is highly recommended that you also include the vocabulary in your course notes. To organize essential vocabulary within your notes, construct the chart below for each vocabulary word you encounter during the lesson.

KEY VOCABULARY WORD	DEFINITION	EXAMPLE OR ILLUSTRATION
Insert the vocabulary word.	*Using your own words, craft a definition of the vocabulary word.*	*Insert an example of the vocabulary word or insert an illustration of the word.*
PICTURE		
Draw a picture that represents the vocabulary word.		

If you have any questions or need additional support with the academic vocabulary for this lesson, be sure to contact your teacher.

After reviewing the template, what are some things that you noticed? Did you see any learning protocols? If so, what were they? Did you also notice that students are defining academic vocabulary using their own words? Additionally, learners are providing examples, illustrations, and even pictorial representations of vocabulary. Why is this important? What's the impact on student instruction?

There are additional ways to support academic language acquisition when designing virtual lessons. With technology, the possibilities are endless. For instance, consider integrating digital flashcards (use Google Docs or Google Slides to create them) that display vocabulary terms, definitions, pictures, and so on. Or incorporate instructional videos that explain and demonstrate the meaning of each term. Such tools and methods can greatly enhance how you present academic vocabulary within your lessons for students.

You might even design student activities that address the lesson's academic vocabulary. In the previous chapter, we examined activities that build vocabulary, such as close passages, survival words, word clouds, a cloud-based word wall, graphic organizers, and the Frayer Model. These tools can also be integrated into this section of the virtual lesson to introduce, grow, and reinforce academic vocabulary. Consider how such activities impact the level of engagement students' experience. Why is that important?

While it's crucial to present academic vocabulary initially, it's equally important to reinforce academic vocabulary throughout the lesson. Consistently and repeatedly reference the academic vocabulary within the lesson you are creating. In fact, each time academic vocabulary is presented within your written text, consider placing it in bold, restating or referencing its definition. If your instructional design software and/ or LMS allows you to hyperlink to other instructional materials, consider hyperlinking each academic vocabulary word directly to a page that houses all definitions for the lesson or course. Similarly, you might use hyperlinks to link to academic websites that define academic vocabulary. As you seek to build academic vocabulary, never forget that remembering requires practice and repetition—so use this strategy when designing your asynchronous lessons.

STOP. REFLECT. PLAN. ACT.

Designing a Virtual Lesson
Academic Vocabulary Section Template

Professional Learning Task. In this section, you examined the importance of presenting and defining the academic vocabulary presented within the virtual lesson. Addressing and building vocabulary supports student comprehension and ultimate achievement of the outcomes for student learning. Now, take a moment to **stop**, **reflect**, **plan**, and **act**. Begin by reviewing the **Virtual Lesson Introduction Academic Vocabulary Template** and other materials in this section. Using the space below, adapt or develop a template for presenting vocabulary within your virtual lessons. Be sure to revisit this template and integrate this framework into practice when designing lessons for your classroom.

Design Essential #4: Deliver Engaging Instruction

The body of the lesson—the fourth and most extensive section—presents new instructional content and materials for learning. While there are various ways to create and deliver virtual content asynchronously, we will focus on designing a written lesson intended to be read by students. The great thing about beginning with this structure is that you can easily integrate additional pictures, charts, videos, examples, activities, and so on to enhance and extend the written lesson you created. Reading also builds comprehension skills in your learners. Additionally, many software design systems offer text-to-speech options to support struggling readers.

Before developing this section, be sure to review the learning outcomes, as they drive the content of the body section. It's also important to consider the lesson content and identify a writing structure that best organizes and presents information to students. Because developing asynchronous, virtual lessons isn't something many of us learned in school, it's important that to delve into specific writing structures that will grow this practice. We identified five common writing structures as a framework for how to organize and present course content. Highlighted in the table below, the structures are categorizing, sequencing, comparing and/or contrasting, evaluating, and causing and effecting.

LESSON WRITING STRUCTURES	
WRITING STRUCTURE	**DESCRIPTION**
Categorizing	Presents information organized by categories, classes, or themes
Sequencing	Presents information sequentially, such as chronologically based upon date and time or even ordered by how tasks are sequenced and completed
Comparing and/or Contrasting	Presents information based upon similarities, differences, or both.
Evaluating	Presents information based upon evaluating a process, action, or decision in relation to specific criteria.
Causing and Affecting	Presents the cause and the effect of a specific phenomenon.

When developing the body section of the lesson, consider which writing structure most effectively organizes and shares the lesson's information and learning targets. To help you, the sections that follow examine how information is presented using each structure.

Writing Structure #1: Categorizing

If information is easily organized into categories, classes, or themes, use the categorizing writing structure to manage your instructional content. For this writing structure, instructional content is presented in the following or a similar structure:

Introducing. Introduce the broad topic of learning and preview all categories, classes, or themes.

Category, Class, or Theme #1. Present the first category, class, or theme and expand upon that concept with specific information, evidence, proof, or other supporting details.

Category, Class, or Theme #2. Present the second category, class, or theme and expand upon that concept with specific information, evidence, proof, or other supporting details. *Note: Continue with each category, class, or theme until all information is presented.*

Concluding. Reintroduce the broad topic of learning and summarize all categories, classes, or themes. Be sure to examine how all categories, classes, or themes intersect. Conclude with a clinching statement compelling continued higher-order thinking.

For instance, suppose you were developing a lesson that introduces government forms in China, Great Britain, and the United States. You might choose to present this information based upon the type of government that exists in each country. In practice, you might organize and offer the instructional content as follows:

- Introducing
- Communist State
- Constitutional Monarchy
- Federal Republic
- Concluding

Why do you think the information was organized by the form of government as opposed to the name of the country? What are the implications of presenting information in this manner?

Writing Structure #2: Sequencing

When determining the appropriate writing structure for your lesson, you will find that some information is best presented sequentially. This can be done chronologically based upon each event's date and time or ordered by the steps required to complete a task. When sequencing events, present the earliest event first and then move forward in time. If outlining steps for a particular task, begin with the first step and end with the last step. In practice, lesson content would be presented as follows:

Introducing. Introduce the broad topic of learning and preview, sequentially, all events or steps associated with a task.

Event or Step #1. Present the first event or step and expand upon that concept with specific information, evidence, proof, or other supporting details.

Event or Step #2. Present the second event or step and expand upon that concept with specific information, evidence, proof, or other supporting details. *Note: Continue with each event or step until all information is presented.*

Concluding. Reintroduce the broad topic of learning and summarize all sequential events or steps. Be sure to examine how all events or steps intersect. Conclude with a clinching statement compelling continued higher-order thinking.

For instance, suppose you were developing a lesson on how to wash your hands. You might organize and present the necessary steps as follows:

- Introducing
- Step One: Turn on the faucet.
- Step Two: Wet your hands.
- Step Three: Add soap and lather.
- Step Four: Rinse.
- Step Five: Dry.
- Concluding

As you are sharing how to perform a task, be sure to expand upon each step with essential information, tips, and strategies. As you begin thinking about structuring a lesson in this way, how might digital images enhance the information you are sharing? What do you foresee as the potential impact on student understanding?

Writing Structure #3: Comparing and/or Contrasting

Comparing and/or contrasting is appropriate when lesson content is examined based upon similarities, differences, or both. Your most important ideas should be presented first, followed by less critical information when using this writing structure. For this writing structure, instructional content is shown in the following or a similar format:

Introducing. Introduce the broad topic of learning and preview the categories that frame the similarities and differences being examined.

Comparing and/or Contrasting Category #1. Present the first similarity or difference and expand upon that idea with specific information, evidence, proof, or other supporting details. *Note: Don't forget to begin with the most critical category or information shared with students.*

Comparing and/or Contrasting Category #2. Present the second similarity or difference and expand upon that idea with specific information, evidence, proof, or other supporting details. *Note: Continue with each category until all information is presented.*

Concluding. Reintroduce the broad topic of learning and summarize all categories. Be sure to examine how all categories intersect. Conclude with a clinching statement compelling continued higher-order thinking.

For example, suppose your lesson examines the similarities and differences of life today and life during the 1800s. To organize and present this information within your lesson, you might structure information as follows:

- Introducing
- In terms of homelife…
- In terms of profession…
- In terms of communication…
- In terms of transportation…
- Concluding

For each category presented above, you'd share similarities as well as differences between life today and life during the 1800s. Take a second to consider this particular writing style. How might this structure be leveraged to share similarities and differences without drawing conclusions for your students? What impact might this have on student learning? How would this impact the design of your assessment?

Writing Structure #4: Evaluating

It might be essential to evaluate a process, action, or decision as part of the instructional lesson. If this is the case, the evaluating writing structure is appropriate. With this particular writing structure, it's imperative to offer information, evidence, proof, or other supporting details within your lesson. In practice, lesson content would be presented as follows:

Introducing. Introduce the broad topic of learning and preview all evaluative categories.

Evaluating Category #1. Present the first evaluative category and expand upon that idea with specific information, evidence, proof, or other supporting details.

Evaluating Category #2. Present the second evaluative category and expand upon that idea with specific information, evidence, proof, or other supporting details. *Note: Continue with each evaluative category until all information is presented.*

Concluding. Reintroduce the broad topic of learning and summarize all evaluative categories. Be sure to examine how categories are interrelated. Conclude with a clinching statement compelling continued higher-order thinking.

As an example, consider a lesson addressing gun control in a high school government course. You might structure your lesson as follows:

- Introducing
- Arguments for Gun Control
- Arguments Against Gun Control
- Those Still Undecided
- Concluding

Take a second to review the structure of this lesson. What do you notice? Does the format promote consideration of all points of view? Is that important? What are the implications for student learning?

Writing Structure #5: Causing and Affecting

The final writing structure, causing and affecting, is appropriate when presenting lesson content on a specific phenomenon. Specifically, what is the phenomenon, and what are the primary causes of the phenomenon? Moreover, what is the impact or effect of that particular phenomenon? In practice, lesson content would be presented as follows:

Introducing. Introduce the broad topic of learning (the phenomenon) and preview the causes and effects associated with the phenomenon.

Causing. Present the causes associated with the phenomenon and expand upon those ideas with specific information, evidence, proof, or other supporting details.

Affecting. Present the effects of the phenomenon and expand upon those ideas with specific information, evidence, proof, or other supporting details.

Concluding. Reintroduce the broad topic of learning and summarize all causes and effects of the phenomenon. Be sure to examine the impact of the phenomenon you are exploring. Conclude with a clinching statement compelling continued higher-order thinking.

Suppose you were designing a lesson on global climate change and marine life. When constructing your lesson, the content might be presented as follows:

- Introducing
- Causes of Global Climate Change
- Impact of Global Climate Change on Marine Life
- Concluding

As you reflect on this lesson's structure, are there ways to make connections to real-world careers? What about a marine biologist? How might you highlight this profession while also connecting to the lesson on global climate change and marine life? What are the implications of doing so? What's the value added?

Other Writing Essentials

Have you ever read something and, when you were done, had no idea what the author was trying to communicate to the reader? Writing effectively can be challenging for many people. It takes time, but like any other skill, the more you practice, the better you get.

When developing an online lesson, at least half of the content tends to be in written form, so as the lesson builders, you need to master best practices for writing. Well-crafted instructional materials support student comprehension and communication skills. The "mechanics" of writing—grammar, organization, and clarity—are fundamental when constructing an online lesson for your blended course, and all of these elements contribute to effectively communicating information to students in an understandable way. The following writing essentials will enhance your lesson design as you begin crafting your online lesson's written elements.

WRITING ESSENTIALS	
ESSENTIAL	**DESCRIPTION**
Exercise Proper Grammar	Develop your lesson with grammar fundamentals in mind. This requires using proper grammar and reviewing and editing your lesson with a critical eye. Be sure that all sentences begin with a capital letter and end with the correct punctuation. You should use complete sentences (sentence form) only. Look for and correct any misspelled words. Be sure to capitalize all proper nouns. Always align verb tenses so they agree.
Use Sentence Form	Words come together to form sentences. Use proper sentence form when developing your lesson. Sentence form refers to the structure and grammatical features of a sentence. Sentence form requires a subject, a verb, and sometimes an object. Typically, the subject is a noun or a person, place, or thing. The verb, or predicate, usually follows the noun. Verbs identify an action or a state of being. Finally, the object receives the action and typically follows the verb. Sentence form also demands the use of proper punctuation. Punctuation refers to the symbols used to separate sentences, distinguish sentence elements, and the structures that offer clarity in writing.

Continued

WRITING ESSENTIALS

ESSENTIAL	DESCRIPTION
Apply Paragraph Form	Paragraph form is also critical. Paragraph form is the structuring of a group of sentences organized by a specific topic or idea. A properly constructed paragraph includes the following types of sentences presented in the following order: • Introductory Sentence (Main Idea) • Supporting Sentence or Sentences • Concluding Sentence An introductory sentence summarizes the main idea of the paragraph. Supporting sentences serve two functions: supporting or proving as well as explaining or expanding upon the topic or main idea. The concluding sentence offers closure by linking all your sentences and ideas together. The concluding sentence may also serve to transition from the ideas presented in your paragraph to the ideas presented in the next paragraph or section. When considering paragraph form, also remember that a paragraph, at minimum, must include three complete sentences. Well-constructed paragraphs have between five and seven sentences.
Use Active Voice	Use active voice (in present, past, or future tense) whenever possible. With active voice, the subject performs the action of the verb. Active voice uses fewer words, allowing you to communicate information clearly and concisely. The following are examples of active voice using present, past, and future tenses: • Present: I tour. • Past: I toured. • Future: I will tour. For comparison, review the below examples of passive voice: • Present Perfect: I have toured. • Past Perfect: I had toured. • Future Perfect: I will have toured. When comparing active and passive voice, what did you notice? Which form requires fewer words? What impact does that have on clarity and conciseness?

Continued

WRITING ESSENTIALS	
ESSENTIAL	**DESCRIPTION**
Integrate Transitions	Transition words and phrases are used to show contrast, illustration, continuation, and conclusion. Here are examples of each type as well as example words and phrases: • Contrast: *however, but, yet, on the other hand,* and *whereas* • Illustration: *first, second, third, for example, for instance,* and *in fact* • Continuation: *furthermore, moreover,* and *coincidentally* • Conclusion: *finally, in conclusion, so, therefore,* and *thus* Use transition words to make connections between the paragraphs within your lesson.
Use Parallel Form	When developing your lesson, use parallel form. This means expressing similar parts of a sentence consistently. The following are examples of parallel form: • Jesse loves **the** sun, **the** sand, and **the** sea. • Kelby **had the** personality, **had the** contacts, and **had the** intelligence to succeed in almost any business venture. Here are examples where parallel form wasn't considered: • Jesse loves the sun, sand, and the sea. • Kelby had the personality, the contacts, and intelligence to succeed in almost any business venture. What are the differences between each example? What impact does the use of parallel form have on clarity and understanding? How does this affect student learning?
Organize Lists	Be consistent in how you list items in your lesson. First, consider whether the information is ordered or unordered. For items that are ordered sequentially, organize the list using numerals (1, 2, 3, and onward). For items where the sequence is irrelevant, use a bullet mark or another mark denoting significance or importance to organize information. Don't forget to be consistent throughout your lesson with how you present ordered and unordered lists.

Continued

WRITING ESSENTIALS	
ESSENTIAL	DESCRIPTION
Present Numbers Consistently	Numbers can be presented in numerical as well as written form. When constructing a lesson, how numbers are expressed should be consistent. In most non-mathematical courses, numbers nine or less are spelled out. Numbers 10 or greater are presented in numerical form. However, when starting a sentence with a number, always use the written form version. For instance, "Nine students attended the virtual field trip."
Select a Citation Style	When developing lessons, it's essential to select a uniform style for citing all works consulted and cited. Words, ideas, pictures, graphics, and so on that aren't your original work should be sourced. The most popular citation styles include the following: • Modern Language Association (MLA) Style (mla.org) • American Psychological Association (APA) Style (apa.org) • *The Chicago Manual of Style* (CMOS) (chicagomanualofstyle.org) For more information on each citation style, be sure to visit the associated websites.

Design Essential #5: Provide Opportunities to Self-Assess and Automated Feedback for Students

When designing virtual lessons, it is essential to embed opportunities for students to self-assess their levels of understanding and opportunities to use automated feedback to determine the progression of learning—the fifth Design Essential. Including short practice assessments or self-assessments encourages students to stop, review, assess, and reflect upon their current understandings (Palloff & Pratt, 2009). Self-assessment data allows students to modify and to refine their knowledge or skills (task, process, or strategy).

The lesson's culminating assessment should not be the first time that students engage with and apply their learning from the lesson. Embedding practice or self-assessment opportunities conditions and prepares students for the final lesson assessment. Because most virtual lessons are asynchronous and on-demand, it's crucial to integrate checks for understanding with automated grading and feedback. Integration of automatic feedback helps students determine their level of knowledge or skill and modify, if appropriate, to meet the lesson's outcomes. Automated grading and feedback features are most prevalent with select-response items or items requiring students to choose their answer from two or more options (Popham, 2008). Still, there are additional ways to assess and automate feedback. The following chart presents self-assessment questioning strategies that typically have automated feedback options within most lesson design software packages.

SELF-ASSESSMENT QUESTIONING STRATEGIES	
STRATEGY	DESCRIPTION
Fill in the Blank	Fill-in-the-blank questions present a sentence or paragraph with a missing word, number, symbol, or phrase. Fill-in-the-blank questions help students recall information presented or apply knowledge or skill to determine and input the correct answer. The benefit of this question type is that students must generate their own answers (Popham, 2008).
Digital Flashcards	Digital flashcards include information, questions, or graphical representations on both sides of the card. Flashcards are useful for helping students memorize or recall such information as vocabulary, definitions, themes, topics, or phrases.
Labeling a Graphic	Some lesson design packages allow you to upload a graphic that learners can identify and label with predetermined answer options. This assessment tool moves beyond simply remembering to actually demonstrating comprehension.
Matching Items	Matching questions allow students to connect words, ideas, and meanings from the lesson. Matching items present two separate lists of words, numbers, symbols, or phrases with one choice from the first list matching one option from the second (Popham, 2008). Matching questions determine a learner's ability to recall specific knowledge or information found in the lesson.

Continued

SELF-ASSESSMENT QUESTIONING STRATEGIES	
STRATEGY	**DESCRIPTION**
Multiple Choice	Multiple-choice questions provide stems with students selecting the correct response from three or more options (Popham, 2008). The benefit to multiple-choice questioning is the ability to design problems that require students to determine the right or best answer option while engaging in higher-order thinking (analysis, synthesis, and evaluation). For example, multiple-choice questions can offer several correct answers, with only one option being the best answer (Popham, 2008). Incorporating answers with varying relative degrees of correctness, with one "best" answer, engages students in higher levels of thinking (Popham, 2008).
Sorting	Sorting assessments require students to classify or organize information, questions, or graphical representations into two or more categories. Sorting, if designed correctly, requires students to analyze answers and place answers in the appropriate category.

With each questioning strategy presented above, what did you observe about the level of thinking required? You probably noticed that many of the strategies address lower-order thinking, and few address high-order thinking. Thus, select your question types with intention. When assessing lower-order outcomes for student learning, leverage questioning strategies that align with lower-order thinking. For example, if you want learners to simply recall information, you might use flashcards. But what if higher-order thinking is required by the learning outcome? If you want students to assess the best option from a series of good choices, use multiple-choice questions.

As noted earlier, many software design packages and even learning management systems with lesson design options allow you to embed the above assessment types with automatic grading and feedback functionality. This enables teachers and designers to embed self-assessment opportunities within virtual lessons for students. The automation level depends on the capabilities of the software you use when developing your lessons—so consider this feature when making your ultimate selection.

As you begin designing self-assessment opportunities within your virtual lessons, it's also important to strategically develop automated feedback. Most of the feedback practices used in a brick-and-mortar classroom also apply to automated feedback.

Remember that feedback should guide and prompt thinking—not provide the correct answer without any productive struggle. Consider this as you begin developing automated feedback. The following design tips will also help you get the best out of your automated feedback.

DESIGN TIPS FOR AUTOMATED FEEDBACK		
Design Tip #1	Celebrating Effort	Always celebrate the student's work and effort.
Design Tip #2	Inquiring and Promoting Thinking	For correct answers, offer automated feedback that poses inquiry-based questions requiring higher-order thinking and that extends learning.
Design Tip #3	Sharing Specific Actions	For incorrect answers, never offer the correct answer within your feedback; instead, provide specific actions that lead students toward the right response.
Design Tip #4	Specifying the Knowledge or Skill	Provide, with specificity, the knowledge or skill (task, process, or strategy) the student is working to achieve with the posed question. Using topics, subtopics, concepts, and vocabulary from the lesson will help students target and identify specific areas within the lesson.
Design Tip #5	Anticipating Learning Support Needs	Anticipate areas where students will need extra support. This might entail noting common misconceptions or mistakes made by students. This might further entail linking directly to the lesson areas that address the range and depth of the question. You might even provide links to additional instructional materials and resources for added support.

Self-assessment with automated feedback is a powerful instructional design strategy for lesson development for both online and blended classrooms. This option isn't typically found in a conventional classroom, so be sure to take advantage of these technologies and this strategy for your students. Although automatic feedback requires time and intentionality, once you've incorporated this feature into your lessons, students have the necessary tools to evaluate their learning. Even better, students can leverage the automated feedback features to regulate and modify their understandings of concepts presented within your lesson. This might be a heavy lift on the front end, but integration maximizes your efforts as well as maximizes student learning.

Design Essential #6: Create Closure and Preview the Assessment

Nothing makes a lesson quite as memorable as a good ending. The final section, or conclusion, brings closure and an element of intrigue and surprise to your lesson. Take a moment to consider the grand finish of your favorite childhood movie. How did the film end? What made the ending unique? Do you think the ending was accidental or the intent of the director? Likely, the conclusion was a product of intention and design. The same is true for how you conclude virtual lessons. The lesson ending is a decision about how you leave your students, and you want to leave your students thirsty for more. While there are numerous design strategies to closeout your virtual lessons, here are strategies we like:

- Extending
- Reflecting
- Reinforcing
- Unexpecting
- Unresolving

To help you deliver upon these strategies to pique and engage your learners' interests, take a moment to review the descriptions and examples in the following chart.

LESSON CLOSURE STRATEGIES	
STRATEGY	**DESCRIPTION**
Extending	You can bring closure to a lesson by extending the learning. One way to expand knowledge is by offering connections to everyday life. Consider how the lesson and learning targets intersect with the world around you. Once you've made those connections, extend learning by integrating real-world applications into your lesson's closing. The goal here is to pique learner interest, compelling the student to continue researching and investigating topics from your lesson.
Reflecting	Reflection can bring closure to your virtual lessons while also demanding high levels of metacognitive thinking by students. Reflection challenges students to assess their levels of understanding by engaging in higher-order thinking skills (HOTS). Consider closing your lesson with reflection-based questions that require students to: • Analyze • Apply • Classify • Create • Decide • Evaluate • Explain • Hypothesize • Infer • Organize • Prioritize • Relate
Reinforcing	If the knowledge or skill (task, process, or strategy) presented in the lesson is critical, you might want to close by reinforcing what students learned. Reinforced connections become more robust and more durable (Dirksen, 2016). Achieve reinforcement by summarizing major lesson topics, themes, ideas, and learning targets for your students. Frequent repetition strengthens learning and helps learners commit information to long-term memory. If the lesson covers foundational or even essential information, you might want to use the lesson's closure to reinforce what was shared.

Continued

LESSON CLOSURE STRATEGIES	
STRATEGY	**DESCRIPTION**
Unexpecting	The unexpected is another way to create learner intrigue and surprise as you close your lesson. Like a movie with a plot twist, the unexpected offers a memorable pivot that learners will not soon forget. Consider the lesson's content. What's incredible and surprising? How can you leverage this to create learner intrigue and connections to future lessons?
Unresolving	Most lessons end with resolution. But why do all lessons have to follow this structure? What if a compelling lesson ends with unresolved learning, questions, and loose ends? What are the implications for student learning? What about student curiosity? When applied correctly, unsettled learning can pique students' interests, leaving them eager to seek answers and continue learning. Unresolved learning is another unique strategy for closing your lesson and engaging your students.

While the conclusion brings an ending to the lesson, that's not its only function. The conclusion should also introduce and preview the lesson's culminating assessment. Include the following assessment information in your lesson's closure:

- Assessment Type (project, essay, debate, and so on)

- Assessment Access (how to access and submit the assessment)

- Assessment Value (points or percentages)

- Assessment Rubric (if applicable)

 After offering closure to the lesson, share assessment information. The following downloadable template provides a framework for previewing the lesson's assessment.

VIRTUAL LESSON ASSESSMENT PREVIEW SECTION TEMPLATE

You did it! You've reached the end of the lesson, and you are ready to show what you know!

You should now be familiar with the concepts presented in the lesson. For lesson *[Insert Lesson Title]*, you will complete a *[Insert Assessment Type]* to determine your understanding. When you are ready, visit your "My Assignments" folder. From there, navigate to the Module *[Insert Module Title]* folder. Then, select the link titled *[Insert Assessment Title]*. The assessment is worth *[Insert Assessment Value]*.

Before completing and submitting the assessment, be sure to complete the following tasks:

- Read the lesson, review all graphics, and watch all instructional videos.

- Finish all learning activities presented within the lesson.

- Take and save detailed notes on major topics and subtopics.

- Review all assessment instructions before beginning the assignment.

- Refresh your memory—before completing the assessment—by reviewing your notes from the lesson.

- As you are working on the assessment, be sure to save your work often.

If you have any questions about the assignment, do not hesitate to contact your teacher.

STOP. REFLECT. PLAN. ACT.

Designing a Virtual Lesson
Assessment Preview Section Template

Professional Learning Task. In this section, you reviewed an example template for previewing the assessment within a virtual lesson. Take a moment to **stop**, **reflect**, **plan**, and **act**. Begin by reviewing the **Virtual Lesson Assessment Preview Template** and other materials in this section. Using the space below, adapt or develop a template for previewing assessments that work best for you. Don't forget to reference your template when designing lessons.

Conclusion

In this chapter, we've examined several instructional design strategies to create captivating virtual lessons for your students. You discovered the importance of organizing and sequencing lessons toward establishing consistency and routines for asynchronous, online learning. You explored how to engage students with self-assessment questions that offer automated feedback, thereby allowing them to self-regulate their understandings. Take a moment to consider the key takeaways from this chapter. What actions will you take toward improved practice? How will your actions ultimately increase student learning? Going forward, how will you leverage designing and deploying asynchronous virtual lessons to address the distinct learning needs of your students? How might this work address challenges associated with learning disruption?

Reflecting for Professional Growth

- What, if any, impact does lesson consistency have on student learning?

- Does each section of the lesson build upon the next? Is the sequence of the framework logical, and if not, what changes would you make?

- How do you currently introduce academic vocabulary in your virtual lessons? Can any of those strategies be adapted when developing online lessons?

- What are some additional ways you can activate prior knowledge when designing virtual lessons?

- Why use writing structures when developing virtual lessons?

- What are your current writing practices? Are there opportunities for growth? If so, what are they?

- What impact do self-assessment opportunities and automated feedback have on student learning?

- How might the lesson opening and closing strategies be adapted for in-person instruction?

- How can you leverage asynchronous, online lessons to meet the individualized and personalized learning needs of your students?

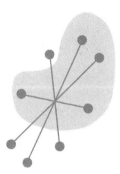

Engaging Students with Authentic Assessments

Outcomes for Professional Learning

In this chapter, we'll discuss:

- Explaining how authentic assessments support deeper learning
- Sharing strategies for formative assessments
- Offering strategies for formal assessments
- Creating an assessment plan

CONNECTING TO THE ISTE STANDARDS FOR EDUCATORS

The content of this chapter relates to the following indicators:

Designer (2.5.a) Educators use technology to create, adapt and personalize learning experiences that foster independent learning and accommodate learner differences and needs.

Analyst (2.7.a) Educators provide alternative ways for students to demonstrate competency and reflect on their learning using technology.

Analyst (2.7.b) Educators use technology to design and implement a variety of formative and summative assessments that accommodate learner needs, provide timely feedback to students and inform instruction.

Analyst (2.7.c) Educators use assessment data to guide progress and communicate with students, parents and education stakeholders to build student self-direction.

I (Nathan) enjoy gardening. Each gardening tool—gloves, a hat, a hoe, a pitchfork—is designed for a specific purpose. A rake is good for moving soil, for example, and a garden trowel is good for digging small holes. Although tools are an important part of the process, so much more goes into creating and cultivating a fruitful garden. You also need the right combination of materials, such as compost, fertilizer, water, and sunlight. You need to sow seeds at certain times of the year, and the soil temperature and pH affect the growth of your fruits or vegetables.

We like to use the metaphor of a garden to show how assessment fits into a student's learning journey. Like rakes and trowels, assessments are just tools that aid in the formative process of learning. Traditional assessment places a lot of emphasis on end-of-year tests, chapter tests, weekly quizzes, and so on, because those tools are easier to work with, as well as more objective and quantifiable than other strategies. These assessments measure just a select few intelligences, however, and they measure them poorly. They are not the right tool for every job. Providing students with multiple ways to demonstrate knowledge and skills increases engagement and learning, and provides teachers with more accurate understanding of students' knowledge and skills.

Authentic assessments provide opportunities for students to learn at a deeper and richer level and to engage with the world around them.

What are some ways you can authentically assess students, while continuing to also provide a process to nurture creativity and critical thinking? Some of our favorite authentic assessments include:

- Reflective video journals

- Debating an issue

- Role playing

- Designing a solution to a problem

- Creating a product

- Peer critique

With these kinds of authentic assessments, we not only put students in charge of their learning; we also get important information that can help us plan for targeted instruction.

FROM THE FIELD
New Formative Assessment Approach

During the remote learning period, Gymea Technology High in New South Wales, Australia, adopted an "anywhere, anytime" approach to teaching and learning that epitomized the transformation underway in assessments. The school developed a new whole-school, continuous formative assessment and homework program around learning platforms, vodcasts, and a Remote Learning Markbook developed in-house that tracked every student's engagement and progress. Students received weekly learning packages that included a set number of targeted, online activities that they worked through at their own pace. Senior students continued with the syllabus via vodcasts produced by Gymea's teachers, which mapped to online tasks such as quizzes, practice exam questions, and draft exam essays. Drawing from data collected by the school's Remote Learning Markbook, individualized emails were sent weekly to students and parents about student progress. Parents will eventually be able to access the data being collected by Gymea's online Student Task Tracker by using individualized logins. The new practices have worked so well that Gymea Tech has retained them now that it has returned to face-to-face teaching. The new formative assessment strategy has created a culture of high expectations for academic achievement and engagement.

---------------------------------•

Measuring Learning with Assessments

To effectively gather evidence of student learning, you first need to understand the two main types of assessments: summative and formative. *Summative assessments,* such as unit tests, are generally given at the conclusion of learning and enable teachers to reliably record student data, provide feedback on their work, and create dynamic portfolios of student progress and growth. *Formative assessment* is a process of gathering evidence as a part of instruction to inform teaching and learning. Two key words in that definition distinguish formative assessments from summative assessments: process and inform.

Unlike summative assessments, formative assessments are used while the learning is taking place: at the beginning of a lesson, in whole-group or small-group checks, or during closure. Another characteristic of formative assessment is that it provides teachers with insight about what students need, which can guide future instructional strategies. By using the information gathered from students on their current level of understanding and reflecting on the end goal, teachers can design instructional pathways that enhance the learning process for each student. Formative assessments make it possible for teachers to take action during, as opposed to after, learning, and can help teachers answer questions about their students, such as:

- Which students are showing gaps in their learning?

- Which students are responding to strategies?

- Which students are not responding to strategies?

- Which students are showing proficiency with learning objectives?

Formative assessments are similar to a mapping app or car navigation system. By using the current location and proposed destination, the app offers several routes for the journey. Along the journey, if you take a turn that wasn't on the proposed plan, the system reroutes and creates new pathways to the original destination. With intentional moments of formative assessments, teachers can do the same for their students.

In some classes teachers use assessments only as evaluation tools to quantify students' current status relative to specific knowledge and skills. Although this is certainly a legitimate use of assessments, we believe their primary purpose should be to provide students with feedback they can use to improve their knowledge or skill. When teachers are intentional with assessments and assessments are directly connected to the level of rigor required by the standard, students understand how their "scores" relate to their status on specific progressions of knowledge and skill they are expected to master.

Engaging Students with Portfolios, Performance Tasks, and Products

Performance tasks and portfolios inform teaching and learning while using strategies that take a comprehensive snapshot of where a student is in their learning. The following table provides an overview of three key summative assessment strategies to use in your classes.

SUMMATIVE ASSESSMENT STRATEGIES	
STRATEGY	DESCRIPTION
Performance Tasks	Performance tasks are a form of assessment that prompt students to research and analyze information, weigh evidence, and solve meaningful problems, allowing them to demonstrate their new learning.
Digital Learning Portfolios	A digital learning portfolio is a dynamic assessment that allows students to demonstrate performance through web-based tools. Learning portfolios can take the form of a website, blog, or video documentary just to name a few.
Student-Created Products	A product is an artifact created by a student that is a culmination of the cognitive and collaborative processes inside of a project or unit.

Performance Tasks

Performance tasks are learning experiences that allow students to evaluate their thinking through a solution path that most resonates with their personal learning modality and represents their current level of thinking about a concept. Performance tasks are often used for math and science classes, but you can use them in any subject area. Because they build on previously learned skills and concepts and require students to synthesize them in ways that make sense in the context of real-world learning, performance tasks make an effective summative assessment.

Performance tasks are not simply bookends to a lesson, however; they are authentic and therefore should be integrated naturally into the learning context. When instruction is focused on learning dispositions (how students behave when engaged in learning), performance task assessments will be more integral to the learning environment because of the natural connection to instruction.

Learning Portfolios

Learning portfolios have taken a new shape in the digital age. They provide students a fun and innovative way of self-documenting and showcasing their learning through the creation of websites, videos, and blog posts. Learning portfolios not only provide an effective means of authentic assessment for you, but give parents, other students, and community members a window into rigorous and relevant learning.

Zubizarreta (2004) stressed the importance of an effective framework for facilitation of student products and portfolios, pointing out the importance of specifically aligning the learning portfolio to learning objectives and goals. The representation of student work, or products, is linked to the reflective and recursive components of the learning portfolio, and it is driven by purpose (real-world application of concepts) and audience (authentic audience in addition to the teacher). Learning portfolios can also serve as a "final product" during an inquiry-based or project-based learning experience. Because this assessment strategy closely emulates real-world work, students are highly motivated and become true curators of their own learning. This approach is also beneficial in providing the data you need to offer appropriate feedback on current levels of learning.

Student-Created Products

Products are often thought of as tangible objects that students build in response to a project assigned by the teacher. They are often a culmination of weeks' worth of collaborating with other students. In fact, a product can be any tangible artifact that students produce (individually or in teams) that thoroughly assesses student knowledge and understanding of subject-area content (products are assessed for evidence of standards). In the "Designing Engaging and Authentic Assessments" section, we will describe some examples of authentic products that make engaging and authentic assessments.

Effective Formative Assessments

Formative assessments help you monitor student progress so you can better differentiate instruction, reteach concepts and skills, address misconceptions, and provide meaningful feedback. The following table offers examples of formative assessment strategies to apply in blended, in-person, or even online learning environments.

EFFECTIVE FORMATIVE ASSESSMENT STRATEGIES	
STRATEGY	DESCRIPTION
Emoji	Provide students with a table or chart that shows the learning objectives or success criteria. Students self-assess where they are with the objective by placing an emoji to indicate their assessment. A smiley emoji could indicate they are feeling good about it. A mind-blown emoji could indicate they are confused about the concept. Decide as a class which emojis you'll use to represent different levels of proficiency.
Virtual Exit Tickets	This simple assessment tool allows students to quickly create a response to a question or a prompt posed by the teacher at the end of a learning block. Vary these tickets by using an online form or having students record a video of themselves sharing their thinking.
Guided Reciprocal Peer Questioning Using Probing Questions	This strategy allows students to develop questions about new learning by creating open-ended probing questions or choosing them from a list. Place questions on a shared collaborative document or slides.

Continued

EFFECTIVE FORMATIVE ASSESSMENT STRATEGIES	
STRATEGY	DESCRIPTION
RSQC2 (Recall, Summarize, Question, Comment, Connect)	This five-step activity guides students quickly through a simple recall, summary, analysis, evaluation, and synthesis exercise. This assessment gives students an opportunity to draw upon new learning while also recalling previous concepts that were scaffolded into the current concept.
KWLs	A KWL (Know, Want to Know, Learned) chart allows you to find out students' prior knowledge on a particular topic. You can then adapt your lessons based on this information. Students can complete the KWL chart when starting a new topic and add to it throughout the unit. Further, the tool helps you see what the students have learned by the end of their lessons.
Think-Pair-Share	Think-Pair-Share is a strategy in which you pose a statement or ask a question of the class. Each student is given time to think and write down their answer. They each then pair up with another student to discuss their answers. After they have had a chance to discuss their answers amongst themselves, they share their answers with a larger group or the rest of the class. You can circulate through the class (or join online small group breakouts) while students are paired in discussion to determine understanding.
Carousel Brainstorming (also called Gallery Walk or World Cafe)	Split the class into groups of four or five students (using your Google Meet or Zoom dashboard, for example), and provide each group with their own online collaborative whiteboard. Have each group write down what they know about a topic or possible answers to an open-ended question. Specify a time limit, and when it's up, have each group pass their whiteboard another group. If you set up multiple boards in Google Jamboard, for example, just ask students to progress to the next board in the sequence. Students must read what the other groups have recorded for answers and then add to the list. They can also circle or highlight answers that they feel hit the mark or add question marks to answers they feel missed the mark.
What Were You Doing?	Take a screenshot or a photo of students during an activity or project. Use those images as writing prompts or discussion starters with the question, "What were you doing in this activity?"

Formative assessments should not only provide you with quick and ongoing checks for understanding, but should also provide students with opportunities to learn while being assessed. Stiggins and Chappuis (2004) called this "assessment FOR learning." During Guided Reciprocal Peer Questioning (GRPQ), students build inquiry skills in the process of question construction while also building metacognition skills through reflection. You can scaffold this strategy by first providing question prompts for students to choose, and then eventually asking students to create their own prompts. To aid in the question generation, refer to the learning protocol of building probing questions. Educator Charlotte Danielson (2011) developed a framework for teaching that included guiding questions. As a guide to get you started using GRPQ, the following example questions can be used as prompts:

- Why do you think this is the case?

- What would you have to change in order for…?

- What do you assume to be true about…?

- How did you conclude…?

- How did your assumptions about…influence how you thought about…?

You can facilitate this process by providing prompts and the appropriate time (ten to fifteen minutes) to conduct this assessment. Another key component of this strategy is capturing student reflection and thinking. This can be enabled through voice recording or collaborative digital documents.

RSQC2 is another formative assessment that builds thinking and learning while also providing you the evidence you need to check for learning. This protocol is unique in that it is structured to emulate the levels of Bloom's Taxonomy. Additionally, the assessment efficacy is higher because it not only focuses on connecting new concepts, but also on building on previously learned concepts. Here are the steps to RSQC2:

Recall. Students make a list of what they recall as most important from a previous learning.

Summarize. Students summarize the essence of previous learning.

Question. Students ask one or two questions that still remain unanswered or that they are unclear of.

Connect. Students briefly explain the essential points and how they relate to their overall math learning goals

Comment. Students evaluate and share feedback about the previous learning.

Assessments provide insights into strengths and weaknesses of student learning. The following graphic provides some example questions you can use to analyze the data you collect. We adapted our examples from the Here's What, So What, Now What protocol (Wellman & Lipton, 2004), which was designed to be completed with colleagues for a team response, whether a district, school, or grade level team.

HERE'S WHAT, SO WHAT, NOW WHAT DATA ANALYSIS PROTOCOL

Adapted from Wellman & Lipton (2004)

Analyze the data from the assessment for the entire grade level or course to address each part of the protocol.

Here's What

What is the data the team needs to be analyzing? Simply recognize the data, categories, and student populations. This is not yet the time to critique or make inferences about student learning in the data.

- Which aspects of our content area should be examined? Strands? Standards? Digital age competencies?

- Which student populations need to be examined for equity in student learning?

- If comparisons are to be made, how should they be made? From teacher to teacher within a grade level? Following a cohort of students?

So What

Recognize trends from the data without yet making inferences or an action plan. Consider using the sentence frame, "I notice..." when articulating observations.

- What do you notice in the data?

- Which content is a strength for students in the grade level or course?

- Which content is a weakness for students in the grade level or course?

Now What

Make conclusions and inferences about the data to structure a collective response to student learning.

- Why might students have scored well or not scored well in light of instructional practices or programs? What will we do about it this year? Next year?

- How do the results show equity or inequity in learning between various student populations? Why? How will we address any inequities this year? Next year?

- Conclude with an action plan and clear role responsibilities for each person involved in analyzing the data.

Designing Engaging and Authentic Assessments

Formative assessments are intended to help students grow in their learning by providing evidence of their proficiency with particular content standards or skills by use of specific feedback. Traditionally, formative assessments come in the form of quizzes, homework, writing prompts, performance tasks, and the like. Although these forms of assessment may provide some evidence of where a student is in relation to a learning target, they are limited in what they measure and can also take the fun out of learning. Every educator knows that lack of engagement has a detrimental effect on student performance.

But what if assessment could be fun and engaging for students? What if it didn't feel like "testing" at all? With this in mind, we suggest having students make video products as a way to engage them in the assessment process. As a formative assessment, video creation illuminates the thinking and learning process, provides opportunities to improve processes and products, and reveals misconceptions along the way. Delivering formative assessment through creativity provides students a motivating environment that supports deeper thinking while giving teachers important data that can be used to inspire subsequent instruction. Not only can reviewing student videos inform and guide your next steps as their teacher, but it can also help students see for themselves how their own ideas integrate, compare, and contrast with those of their peers. Students are able to see how other students may share the same view or level of thinking. The more comfortable students are in sharing those ideas, the more visible they will make their thinking.

Here are some examples of digital products to try with your students:

- PSA informing an audience of a student-created solution

- Historical documentary

- Video presentation (instead of slides)

- Book trailer

- Podcast (audio-only version of multimedia/video)

- Critique/review

- Discussion board

- Timeline

- Proposal

- Project

- Portfolio

- Newsletter

- Editorial

- Video reflection journal

- Interview

Video creation not only serves as an instructional support and learning experience, but as a powerful and effective formative assessment tool. Video creation overcomes several limitations of traditional assessment. Consider the following:

- Video creation opens the door to organically embracing the revision process without students feeling the drudgery of taking a test.

- Students are motivated to revise their work within a video creation project because the results are instantly viewable and encourage further refinement.

- There is an element of gratification that makes the video creation process more welcoming, especially when compared to a paper-and-pencil quiz or test.

- Video creation gives students an outlet for creativity, the output of which the student can feel both proud and invested.

Video Creation as Assessment

Let's walk through a lesson example using a video product as an assessment: A group of students has chosen to research, and in turn engage in critical thinking and creativity, as well as take action on elephant poaching in Africa. Students have a variety of approaches at their disposal through which to demonstrate learning. Options can be as simple as written summaries, but you encourage the students to take more complex, multi-dimensional, and collaborative routes, such as creating videos. Whichever option is taken, students will need to provide formative feedback that is aligned to the learning goal. The first step toward enabling students to guide and track their progress on the way to a learning goal is through a well-defined rubric.

STANDARDS ADDRESSED

ELA Standard: Report on a topic or text, tell a story, or recount an experience with appropriate facts and relevant, descriptive details, speaking clearly at an understandable pace.

ISTE Standards for Students, Creative Communicator (6a) Students choose the appropriate platforms and tools for meeting the desired objectives of their creation or communication.

Developing a Rubric

A rubric is needed to assess complex video products and performance tasks. But rubrics should also be used throughout a unit/project as a tool for guiding students as they work. Introduce rubrics near the beginning, when students hear about (or help decide) what the major products of the project will be. When you share a rubric say, "Here's how you'll be assessed." Have students either practice using the rubric several times or co-create a rubric and then practice using it. To have students practice using a rubric, find some examples of the kind of work required in the project. If students need to write a scientific report after an investigation, show them one—but on a different topic, to prevent direct copying. If they need to design a theater blueprint, show them how to research for other blueprints. You can use the following rubric as a guide for how to assess the elephant poaching lesson.

EXAMPLE RUBRIC			
GOAL	**APPROACHING**	**MEETS EXPECTATIONS**	**ABOVE AND BEYOND**
Criteria #1. Developing a powerful cohesive message through the synthesis of multiple sources and engaging in metacognitive processes.	You have combined a few ideas and some of your own to develop a message that resonates with some. There are some gaps in your story that keep the audience from fully grasping what you're trying to communicate. Your thinking was visibly articulated through application, but not quite reconstructing and synthesizing the concepts into a unified message.	You have broken apart multiple ideas and pieces of evidence from your interviews and a variety of research sources to reconstruct and develop a powerful message that demonstrates thoughtful insight on your topic. Your central message causes the reader to think, "I've never thought of that before" and to want to explore your ideas further. Your thinking was visibly articulated through application and synthesis.	You have broken apart multiple ideas and pieces of evidence from your interviews and a variety of research sources to reconstruct and develop a powerful message that demonstrates thoughtful insight on your topic. Additionally, your synthesis includes powerful digital media that captures the emotions of your audience and clearly communicates a compelling message that conveys the significance of why it's important today. You have inspired your audience to act. Your thinking was visibly articulated through application, synthesis, debate, and evaluation.

Continued

EXAMPLE RUBRIC			
GOAL	APPROACHING	MEETS EXPECTATIONS	ABOVE AND BEYOND
Criteria #2. Historical Context and Applied Relevancy	You provide an accurate, thorough, and relevant historical context for your interviews. There were no primary sources cited in your research. Some of the examples provided don't clearly connect to your central message and there are only loose connections to today's relevance.	You provide an accurate, thorough, and relevant historical context for your interviews, including at least one primary source from research. You include specific examples and evidence to illustrate your points. You clearly make connections from the past to today.	You provide an accurate, thorough, and relevant historical context for your interviews, including at least one primary source from research. You include specific examples and evidence to illustrate your points. You clearly make connections from the past to today. Additionally, you make predictions about future impacts and scenarios given current data and statistical analysis. You also integrate human behavior and psychology into your discussion of the historical context to give your story more credence and strength.

Researching the Topic and Creating an Effective Product

Now let's consider a potential outcome of this project. Teams of students research several topics, including the impact of African elephant poaching on local communities, the international ban on ivory trade, and the history of ivory and its uses. Building on that research:

- Students propose novel solutions to prevent poaching.

- Students use Google Hangouts to chat with other students in Botswana, Tanzania, Zimbabwe, Kenya, Zambia, and South Africa.

- Students work with the World Wildlife Fund and use WeVideo to create a documentary video through which they share their research and the content of their conversations with students in African countries.

- The video contains clips shared by local student eyewitnesses living in the communities that are impacted by elephant poaching.

- To raise awareness, students include cinematic elements and then post the final video project to YouTube.

The assessment is designed to challenge students to think with complexity as they must both research to understand the problem and then evaluate solutions to the matter. Students must analyze multiple sources of data from research and from locals. They then must create a deliverable using an open-ended and iterative process, in this case, video creation, that involves multiple steps. The multiple steps involved in creating the video afford you a window into the progression of student thinking (making thinking visible is truly the most authentic assessment opportunity), which makes it easier to address misconceptions and present new learning opportunities.

Creating an Assessment Plan

Thus far, you have explored the different types of assessment and strategies for implementing them in a blended learning context, and you know assessments must meet the needs of every student. Are there opportunities where one assessment should be used over the other? By using tools that support high levels of aligned assessment, you can create a scaffolded assessment plan that not only captures basic levels of understanding but also students' ability to apply new concepts, analyze information, and solve real-world problems. One tool to help you with this is Norman Webb's (1997) Depth of Knowledge (DOK), which categorizes tasks according to the complexity of thinking required to successfully complete them.

WEBB'S DOK LEVELS

Level 1. Recall and Reproduction: Tasks at this level require recall of facts or rote application of simple procedures. The task does not require any cognitive effort beyond remembering the right response or formula. Copying, computing, defining, and recognizing are typical Level 1 tasks.

Level 2. Skills and Concepts: At this level, a student must make some decisions about their approach. Tasks with more than one mental step, such as comparing, organizing, summarizing, predicting, and estimating, are usually Level 2.

Level 3. Strategic Thinking: At this level of complexity, students must use planning and evidence, and thinking is more abstract. A task with multiple valid responses, where students must justify their choices, would be Level 3. Examples include solving non-routine problems, designing an experiment, or analyzing characteristics of a genre.

Level 4. Extended Thinking: Level 4 tasks require the most complex cognitive effort. Students synthesize information from multiple sources, often over an extended period of time, or transfer knowledge from one domain to solve problems in another. Designing a survey and interpreting the results, creating a brand-new product, analyzing multiple texts to identify and categorize themes, or writing an original myth in an ancient style would all be examples of Level 4.

 In partnership with Webb's DOK levels, Bloom's Taxonomy—and related models—can assist you in developing an effective assessment plan. In practice, teachers assign Bloom's Taxonomy levels according to the main action verb associated with a level in the taxonomy.

Building upon Bloom's early work, many educational and cognitive psychologists have since developed various schemas to describe the cognitive demand for different learning and assessment contexts. In 2001, Anderson and Krathwohl presented a structure for rethinking Bloom's Taxonomy. Whereas the original taxonomy applied one dimension, the revised taxonomy table employs two dimensions: cognitive processes and knowledge. The revised descriptors consider both the processes (the verbs) and the knowledge (the nouns) used to articulate educational objectives. This restructuring of the original taxonomy recognizes the importance of the interaction between the content taught—characterized by factual, conceptual, procedural, and metacognitive knowledge—and the thought processes used to demonstrate learning. You can use the following question stems based on Bloom's levels as you develop your assessment plan. (Scan the QR code for a downloadable list.)

EXAMPLE BLOOMS TAXONOMY QUESTION STEMS

REMEMBERING QUESTION STEMS (LEVEL 1)

- What is...?
- Where is...?
- How did...happen?
- Why did...?
- When did...?
- How would you show...?
- Who were the main...?
- Which one...?

- How is...?
- When did...happen?
- How would you explain...?
- How would you describe...?
- Can you recall...?
- Can you select...?
- Can you list the three...?
- Who was...?

UNDERSTANDING QUESTION STEMS (LEVEL 2)

- How would you classify the type of...?
- How would you compare...?
- How would you contrast...?
- Compare and contrast...
- State or interpret in your own words...
- How would you rephrase the meaning...?

- What facts or ideas show...?
- What is the main idea of...?
- Which statements support...?
- Explain what is happening...
- What is meant...?
- What can you say about...?
- Which is the best answer...?
- How would you summarize...?

APPLYING QUESTION STEMS (LEVEL 3)

- How would you use...?
- What examples can you find to...?
- How would you solve...using what you've learned...?
- How would you organize...to show...?
- How would you show your understanding of...?

- Why did...do or choose..., and why?
- What would you recommend...?
- How would you rate the..., and why?
- What would you cite to defend the actions...?
- How could you determine...?

- What choice would you have made…?

- How would you prioritize…?

- What facts would you select to show…?

- What questions would you ask in an interview with…?

ANALYZING QUESTION STEMS (LEVEL 4)

- What are the parts or features of…?

- How is…related to…?

- Why do you think…?

- What is the theme…?

- What motive is there…?

- Can you list the parts…?

- What inference can you make…?

- What conclusions can you draw…?

- How would you classify…?

- How would you categorize…?

- Can you identify the different parts…?

- What evidence can you find…?

- What is the relationship between…?

- Can you distinguish between…?

- What is the function of…?

- What ideas justify…?

VALUATING QUESTION STEMS (LEVEL 5)

- Do you agree with the actions…? …with the outcome?

- What is your opinion of…?

- How would you prove…? Disprove…?

- Can you assess the value or importance of…?

- Would it be better if…?

- Why did…do or choose…, and why?

- What would you recommend…?

- How would you rate the…, and why?

- What would you cite to defend the actions…?

- How could you determine…?

- What choice would you have made…?

- How would you prioritize…?

- What judgment would you make about…?

- Based on what you know, how would you explain…?

- What information would you use to support the view…?

- How would you justify…?

- What data was used to make the conclusion…?

- Why was it better that…?

- How would you compare the ideas… to…?

CREATING QUESTION STEMS (LEVEL 6)

- What changes would you make to solve…?

- How would you improve…?

- What would happen if…?

- Can you elaborate on the reason…?

- Can you propose an alternative…?

- How would you adapt…to create a different…? How could you change (modify) the plot (plan)…? What could be done to minimize (maximize)…? What way would you design…?

- Can you invent…?

- What could be combined to improve (change)…? Suppose you could… what would you do…? How would you test…?

- Can you formulate a theory for…?

- Can you predict the outcome if…?

- How would you estimate the results for…? What facts can you compile…?

- Can you construct a model that would change…? Can you think of an original way for the…?

Although the tools are related through their natural ties to the complexity of thought, Webb's DOK and Bloom's Taxonomy differ in scope and application, as Hess et al. (2009) eluded to. Depth of knowledge relates more closely to the depth of content understanding and scope of a learning activity, which manifests in the skills required to complete the task from inception to finale (planning, researching, drawing conclusions). Bloom's Taxonomy, on the other hand, categorizes the cognitive skills required of the brain to perform a task, describing the "type of thinking processes" necessary to answer a question. Both the depth of content knowledge and the thinking processes have direct implications in curricular design, lesson delivery, and assessment development and use.

 To help you put these together, we have developed the Assessment Design Plan tool. With this tool, you begin with the big idea of the unit. Then you decide on what the finished product will look like (summative assessment) for students. Because learning is a process, it's important that you develop assessments that match the scaffolding you're providing and are highly aligned to the cognitive domains that are being required. We have included two examples of what this plan could look like for a math and a science unit. The following Assessment Design Plan Template works well for any unit no matter the subject, grade level, or type of learning environment. For additional, downloadable copies, scan the QR code.

ASSESSMENT DESIGN PLAN TEMPLATE

Big Idea/Enduring Understandings:

Formative Assessment	Webb's DOK	Bloom's Level	How Does this Assessment Support the Big Idea?
Final Product/ Summative:			

MATH ASSESSMENT DESIGN PLAN

Big Idea/Enduring Understandings:
A Study in Cooperation: Design a Theater for Your Local Community

Formative Assessment	Webb's DOK	Bloom's Level	How Does this Assessment Support the Big Idea?
Blueprint Sketch (Individual)	Level 2: Students make mock-ups based on other blueprints.	Comprehend	This allows students the opportunity to think of their own ideas before they join a team, with whom they will create one shared model.
Measurement Task/Quiz (Individual)	Level 1: Students demonstrate that they understand the basic measurement skills required to create the scale model.	Apply	This formative ensures students have the foundational measurement skills needed to create an accurate scale model.

Continued

MATH ASSESSMENT DESIGN PLAN

Big Idea/Enduring Understandings:
A Study in Cooperation: Design a Theater for Your Local Community

Formative Assessment	Webb's DOK	Bloom's Level	How Does this Assessment Support the Big Idea?
Gallery Walk (Team)	Level 3: Teams review each other's sketches to decide which components are best to include on the team model. Teams need to explain how they arrived at the decision in preparation for critiques.	Synthesis	Teams are narrowing down their list of ideas to select the most useful design components for community board members.
Scale Model (Individual)	Level 4: Students create a draft using accurate measurement and scaling. Teacher reviews and provides feedback.	Create	Students will have a critiqued draft before creating the physical scale model.
Final Product/ Summative: A Physical Model of the Theater (Team)	Level 4: In teams, students create a scale model of their courtyard redesign to solve a real-world problem and make a pitch to site administration and local architects for their designs.	Create	Mission complete!

SCIENCE ASSESSMENT DESIGN PLAN

Big Idea/Enduring Understandings:
A Study in Human Impacts: Design a Plan to Mitigate E. coli in a Local Lake

Formative Assessment	Webb's DOK	Bloom's Level	How Does this Assessment Support the Big Idea?
Chemical Reactions Task/ Quiz (Individual)	Level 1: Students demonstrate understanding of types of chemical reactions.	Apply	This formative assessment ensures students have the foundational understanding of chemical reactions occurring in the lake.
Water Testing Lab Write-Up (Individual)	Level 3: Students analyze information with data sets and interrelationships between human impacts and the water supply.	Analyze	This allows students to articulate the evidence that will be presented in the video.
Letter to Community Leaders with Results and Recommendations (Team)	Level 3: Students cite evidence and develop logical arguments. Students justify their conclusions.	Evaluate	The arguments and reasoning in this letter will be used to create the video.
Final Product/ Summative: PSA Video Created and Shared on YouTube (Team)	Level 4: After reviewing multiple perspectives and data points, students use their own voice to create a persuasive video articulating their viewpoint.	Create	Mission accomplished!

The last column is important for ensuring that each formative assessment aligns to the overarching idea. How many times do you hear students say, "When are we ever going to need this?" You'll also notice the inclusion of a traditional "quiz" or "task" in the examples. These can be effective, but only when appropriately matched to the cognitive demand required. You wouldn't give an assessment requiring students to use true/false when you want to measure their ability to justify conclusions. But if you want to know if students have recall of basic facts, a selected response would be appropriate.

Conclusion

I (Nathan) was going through some old emails recently and came upon a grad school assignment I sent to my professor a few years ago. The task was to create a video reflection on a leadership project I had been a part of. I created the video and sent it to my professor and also saved it to my YouTube channel. When I rediscovered the video years later, I was not only astonished at how much my Southern accent and vocabulary changed, but also at how much my thinking changed. In the video, I was discussing a particular concept around leadership, and in that moment, I was able to see how my thinking changed over some time. It caused me to wonder, "What led to my shift in thinking?" and "How long did it take to shift my thinking?" It was a pleasant assessment of my shift in thinking and all in thanks to a video I created. When thinking about the true purpose of an assessment, it's important to consider where you were and where you are now. Because of accountability and the continuing push for standardized testing, this perspective of assessments is often concealed.

So, how can we each best see how our perspective and thinking have evolved? A traditional assessment may capture the current level of knowledge retention, but that doesn't tell us anything about our thinking. Our thinking changes (as we grow and learn) over time, and so the question becomes, how do we best illuminate this progression of thinking and learning?

Authentic assessment is a powerful tool that is not only changing the landscape of creativity and student engagement in the classroom, it's changing how educators measure learning. When authentic assessments illuminate students' thinking, students are engaged in metacognition, which means "thinking about thinking." When engaged in metacognition through reflection, students are focused on their current feelings and thoughts. By being mindful of their emotional state, for example, teachers and students can more effectively steer their feelings and thoughts in a more positive "can-do" direction. As they realize the story of their learning, they begin to synthesize how the chunks of new learning all connect.

As we conclude this chapter, we want to leave you with a final authentic assessment: video reflection journals. Video reflection journals might be new to you and/or your students but are easy to use in your classroom. An initial roadblock of video journaling is figuring out what to talk about. We find that if you have a conversation with your class and guide them through a couple of reflection questions, they will soon have lots of talking points.

Here are a few prompts to help get the conversation started:

- When were you on track with this project?

- How did you know you were on track?

- During this project, when were you successful?

- What did that feel/look like?

- When were you most engaged/focused on this project?

- What were you doing? How did that action affect the end result?

Assessing your own thinking is a powerful strategy because you're engaging in high levels of thinking while also getting information about where you are in relation to what you've learned. For students, authentic assessments reveal emotions, tone, and visual representations. If done in a meaningful and thoughtful way it can help students become powerful idea generators and provide a platform for reflective thinking.

Reflecting for Professional Growth

- What makes an assessment authentic?

- How do you ensure your assessments align with the level of rigor or cognitive demand that the learning objective or essential question requires?

- How will the data analysis protocol change how you plan instruction and design assessments?

- What formative assessment strategies will you now implement? What about summative assessment strategies?

- How does reflection serve as an authentic assessment?

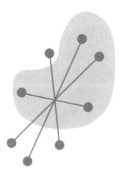

Maximizing
Academic Feedback

Outcomes for Professional Learning

In this chapter, we'll discuss:

- Defining academic feedback

- Integrating quality feedback essentials into practice

- Creating feedback norms

- Evaluating feedback as a formative assessment strategy

- Differentiating feedback based upon the level of understanding

- Integrating feedback protocols into practice

CONNECTING TO THE ISTE STANDARDS FOR EDUCATORS

The content of this chapter relates to the following indicators:

Learner (2.1.a) Educators set professional learning goals to explore and apply pedagogical approaches made possible by technology and reflect on their effectiveness.

Learner (2.1.c) Educators stay current with research that supports improved student learning outcomes, including findings from the learning sciences.

Designer (2.5.b) Educators design authentic learning activities that align with content area standards and use digital tools and resources to maximize active, deep learning.

Designer (2.5.c) Educators explore and apply instructional design principles to create innovative digital learning environments that engage and support learning.

Analyst (2.7.b) Educators use technology to design and implement a variety of formative and summative assessments that accommodate learner needs, provide timely feedback to students and inform instruction.

Feedback has the perception of being a unidirectional bestowal of teacherly knowledge and opinions, wrapped in bias, delivered to students. As the "expert" in the classroom, the teacher is the natural provider of said expertise. We're being a bit tongue-in-cheek here, but many times this is genuinely the way in which feedback is viewed. Similarly, educators often think feedback can ultimately unlock a profound aspect of thinking and learning, but this only happens when you disrupt traditional feedback practices and perceptions. Feedback is much more than telling; academic feedback is a learning process that incorporates the crucial aspect of asking inquiry-based questions. For example, "You said that the local tribes in North Dakota have every right to protest the pipeline. How did you make that conclusion? Do you have prior experiences that influenced your judgment? What specific information, evidence, proof, or other supporting details informed your conclusion?" Such inquiry-based questioning prompts students to examine their thought processes and challenge existing assumptions, beliefs, and ideas toward higher levels of understanding and awareness.

In positive, authentic, and collaborative learning environments, teachers develop a culture of curiosity using reflective dialogue and inquiry. In these environments, teachers are not the only ones responsible for supporting the creation of high-quality student work. Students are as well. In collaborative environments, learners have regular, structured opportunities with the teacher and peers offering, receiving, and collaborating on work in progress and even the larger learning context. Students are taught how to constructively critique one another's work and use feedback to revise and improve their knowledge, task, process, or strategy. Feedback can also be a formative assessment "checkpoint," in which students pause to reflect and provide critiques of each other's work.

Going forward, teachers must be adept at providing quality feedback both synchronously and asynchronously. Hence, being able to develop and refine continually for all settings is a critical teaching skill. In this chapter, we will define and outline the characteristics of quality feedback. In addition, we will discuss tailoring and personalizing feedback based upon student comprehension. We will also explore presenting asynchronous, written feedback when students aren't in person, and we'll examine systems and structures that support cycles of feedback. Once you've completed this chapter, you will have the knowledge, skills, and tools to maximize the impact of academic feedback in your classroom.

Defining Feedback

In *Challenging Learning Through Feedback*, James and Jill Nottingham (2017) described academic feedback as a means to provide information about the knowledge, the task, the process, or the strategy employed by the student. Differentiated feedback helps students close the gap between where they want to be and where they are now. Quality academic feedback supports student thinking by helping teachers and students understand:

- The learning outcome

- Where the student is in relation to the outcome

- What the learner needs to do to bridge the gap between the current position and the learning target (Nottingham & Nottingham, 2017)

In short, quality feedback helps learners answer the following key questions (Nottingham & Nottingham, 2017):

- "What am I trying to achieve?"

- "How much progress have I made so far?"

- "What should I do next?"

Feedback should also address any misconceptions or misunderstandings that students have about their learning. Fisher and Frey (2007) further explained that feedback must be timely, understandable, and actionable. Take a moment to stop, reflect, plan, and act on that thought.

STOP. REFLECT. PLAN. ACT.

Defining Quality Academic Feedback

Professional Learning Task. In this section, you began defining academic feedback. Take a moment to **stop, reflect, plan,** and **act**. In your own words, craft an operational definition of academic feedback to guide future planning and action.

Quality Feedback Essentials

If you survey the research and literature on academic feedback, you will notice that common themes quickly emerge. Most acknowledge that feedback must connect to the knowledge, the process, the task, or the strategy presented in the outcome for student learning. This level of alignment ensures that feedback remains clear, objective, constructive, and tied to the learning outcome. Feedback must also be actionable—allowing learners to make immediate modifications to their knowledge, their process, their task, or their strategy to achieve the outcomes presented. Students need to know where they are in relation to the learning outcome and where they still need to go. It's also important to develop safe, supportive, and collaborative classroom cultures conducive to cyclical, ongoing feedback structures. Finally, researchers agree that simple praise or vague statements about learning doesn't constitute academic feedback.

QUALITY FEEDBACK ESSENTIALS	
Essential #1: Acknowledging and Affirming	Feedback acknowledges the student by name and the student's effort—affirming that feedback is a learning process.
Essential #2: Clear and Specific	Feedback is clear and specific. Feedback reduces uncertainty as to how students perform and what needs to be accomplished to attain mastery.
Essential #3: Actionable and Active	Feedback is actionable and useable by the learner. Students should be actively using feedback as opposed to passively receiving feedback and never taking action to improve their learning.
Essential #4: Differentiated	Feedback is appropriately challenging and differentiated based upon the student's level of understanding.
Essential #5: Objective	Feedback focuses on the knowledge, task, process, or strategy presented in the learning outcome. Feedback is objective and unbiased.
Essential #6: Timely	Feedback is timely, offered during or quickly after consequential learning.
Essential #7: Supportive	Feedback is offered within a culture of trust, respect, and support. Feedback allows for learning from mistakes rather than making students fear failure. This includes emphasizing that effort leads to increased learning and that mistakes are vital to the learning process.
Essential #8: Reinforcing	Feedback reinforces helping students identify what they have done correctly to determine better what they can do next.
Essential #9: Cues	Feedback offers supportive cues that center on knowledge, task, process, or strategy.

So how do you define quality feedback? What essential elements or strategies have you identified? Which of these practices do you currently use? The previous chart presents the essentials we've identified; use it to assess alignment with your existing feedback practices and improve them as you continue reimagining instruction in your classroom.

During the pandemic, much of the feedback provided to learners was asynchronous, written feedback. Building relationships from a distance is challenging, but knowing your students and addressing them by their names is a good beginning. Build on this by making feedback an active, not passive, process where students are expected to use and act upon the relayed information. Again, offering written feedback during the pandemic quickly taught us all that feedback has value only if students actually use and apply it. Thus, many teachers integrated practices that required students to integrate feedback to improve or adjust their learning in some way.

Take a moment to evaluate your current feedback practices and consider how to integrate some new strategies into your practice.

STOP. REFLECT. PLAN. ACT.

Quality Feedback Essentials

Professional Learning Task. In this section, you began identifying characteristics of high-quality feedback. Using the chart below, **stop**, **reflect**, **plan**, and **act** upon your learning.

3	Identify three feedback essentials that you discovered in this section.	1. 2. 3.
2	Outline how you plan to integrate two of those essentials into professional practice.	1. 2.
1	Consider improving the characteristics of quality feedback by developing one essential item that is missing from the list.	1.

As discussed, it's important to establish norms around how learners will review and use your written feedback for resubmission purposes; otherwise, the feedback may be ineffective. For instance, when they resubmit work, you might require students to:

1. Review the written feedback, along with the grade, carefully.

2. Use the feedback to revise the learning product.

3. Submit the revised work and answer the question, "How did you use the feedback to improve the quality of the subsequent submission?"

This three-step process is essential. If students aren't actively using your feedback, then your hard work and effort are wasted.

Feedback Norms

Teacher feedback should occur throughout the learning process and include frequent opportunities for students to provide feedback to peers to improve their learning products. This includes self-assessment as well. There are many junctures for students and teachers to offer feedback, such as during lessons, small-group activities, individual conversations, product work sessions, and so on. Feedback shouldn't be narrowed to only summative assessments or significant writing assignments. Instead, feedback should be part of the culture of your classroom.

Developing a feedback culture requires intentionality, planning, and clear norms for engagement. *Norms* are customs, habits, as well as expectations for how things operate within a group. Clearly defined norms help students achieve the goals and outcomes you've established, and Berger, Rugen, and Woodfin (2014) noted that formal and informal feedback must be grounded in the norms you've established for your class. To build and sustain a culture for feedback, they recommend you establish norms that are:

*   Kind

*   Specific to knowledge, skill, process, or task

*   Helpful

Berger, Rugen, and Woodfin (2014) also highlighted that "norms are kind." You must create a positive, safe, and supportive culture around offering and receiving feedback. Without this foundation, the success of this learning process will be at risk of failing. So, begin by creating or sustaining positive, safe, and supportive feedback norms.

Teacher-to-student feedback and student-to-student feedback is a form of communication, and effective communication requires mastery of both listening and speaking skills. Hence, your feedback norms for students must address both listening and speaking. For instance, norms might require that students don't just casually listen. Students must closely listen with their undivided attention and without interruption. Likewise, speaking norms may entail a specific protocol for communicating feedback to others, a protocol that supports detailed, clear, and actionable feedback connected to the outcomes for student learning.

Take a moment to consider what you've learned about feedback and learning norms. How will you design clear norms for engaging with academic feedback? Stop, reflect, plan, and act upon your ideas.

STOP. REFLECT. PLAN. ACT.

Feedback Norms

Professional Learning Task. In this section, you began reviewing norms for engaging students in the feedback process. Using the space below, **stop**, **reflect**, **plan**, and **act** upon your learning. Devise ten overarching norms that will guide you and your students' feedback expectations and engagement practices. Also, consider when and how to share norms with students.

1.

2.

3.

4.

5.

Feedback as a Formative Assessment Strategy

Providing students with quality formative feedback during the learning process engages higher-order thinking and increases student comprehension and understanding. Yet John Hattie and Gregory Yates (2014) point out that research indicates an "empathy gap" in students' and teachers' perceptions of formative feedback. Teachers believe they regularly provide valuable feedback, yet student perceptions and outside observer ratings indicate otherwise (John Hattie and Gregory Yates, 2014). Feedback is an effective formative assessment strategy, but only when students have opportunities to revise and improve their work. In other words, it is an effective strategy when the feedback is active and actionable. The following chart distinguishes and characterizes feedback quality and impact when used as a formative assessment tool.

EVALUATING FEEDBACK AS A FORMATIVE ASSESSMENT STRATEGY		
Adapted from Nyquist, 2003		
PERFORMANCE LEVEL	**CATEGORY**	**DESCRIPTION**
Higher-Order Thinking Skills (HOTS)	Extremely Effective Formative Feedback	Students receive their grades, the correct answers, as well as specific, actionable, and differentiated feedback on knowledge, task, process, or strategy for improvement purposes. Feedback is also directly linked to the outcomes for student learning.
	Effective Formative Feedback	Students receive their grades, the correct answers, as well as some explanations and suggestions for improvement.
	Moderately Effective Formative Feedback	Students receive their grades, the correct answers, as well as some information for improvement purposes.
	Ineffective Formative Feedback	Students receive their grades plus information about possible correct answers.
Lower-Order Thinking Skills (LOTS)	Extremely Ineffective Formative Feedback	Students receive their grades.

What caught your attention in the chart? Consider that when teachers only provide grades, the learning stops. As feedback becomes more specific and actionable, what impact does that have on student learning? Effective feedback requires students to go deeper. That's the power of quality, actionable feedback: The learning continues.

STOP. REFLECT. PLAN. ACT.

Evaluating Feedback as a Formative Assessment Strategy

Professional Learning Task. In this section, you evaluated feedback as a formative assessment strategy. Take a moment to **stop**, **reflect**, **plan**, and **act**. Consider the relationship between feedback that identifies detailed knowledge, task, process, or strategy in relation to the student's performance level. Consider how extremely effective formative feedback promotes higher-order thinking in students.

Differentiating Feedback

Providing quality feedback is one of the most critical roles of a teacher, and that feedback has the potential to improve student comprehension and understanding dramatically. Quality feedback is specific, actionable, and differentiated, addressing knowledge, task, process, or strategy. But how exactly do you differentiate feedback for your students? James and Jill Nottingham (2017) developed the Structure of Observed Learning Outcomes (SOLO) Taxonomy model to help teachers personalize feedback based on a student's level of understanding. The SOLO method is a means of classifying the complexity of the student's knowledge toward individualizing the scope and depth of the feedback provided to the learner. The SOLO method offers a practical framework for matching academic feedback to a student's stage of learning. The following table presents each of the five SOLO levels, defines the level of understanding, and gives example feedback verbs for inquiry-based questioning.

SOLO TAXONOMY MODEL *Adapted from Nottingham & Nottingham, 2017*		
SOLO LEVEL	**LEVEL OF STUDENT UNDERSTANDING**	**EXAMPLE ACTION VERBS FOR INQUIRY-BASED FEEDBACK**
Prestructural The student has no idea.	No Idea	Too soon for feedback, as direct instruction is needed first
Unistructural The student has one idea.	Idea	• Find • Match • Label • Name • List
Multistructural The student has many ideas.	Ideas	• Describe • Define • Combine • Follow • Identify
Relational The student understands the whole.	Related Ideas	• Classify • Analyze • Relate • Apply • Explain • Organize
Extended Abstract The student can predict and invent.	Extended Ideas	• Evaluate • Prioritize • Hypothesize • Create

How does the level of understanding presented in the SOLO Taxonomy model impact the type of feedback you offer to your students? When is it appropriate to bypass academic feedback and provide direct instruction to the student? When offering asynchronous feedback, many teachers face this situation. How do you address this challenge? What works and doesn't work for students? Also consider, if a student understands many of the lesson's ideas, how might you personalize their feedback? How might you continue to challenge their thinking with the feedback that you offer?

What inquiry-based verbs would you use when crafting such feedback? Leveraging the SOLO Taxonomy model allows you to differentiate your feedback and questioning strategies, challenging learners to higher levels of comprehension and understanding.

STOP. REFLECT. PLAN. ACT.

SOLO Taxonomy Model

Professional Learning Task. In this section, you investigated how to differentiate academic feedback for students. Take a moment to **stop**, **reflect**, **plan**, and **act** upon your learning. Until you are familiar with and regularly using the SOLO Taxonomy model, what three actions will you take to embed this into your professional practice?

1.

2.

3.

Feedback Protocols

During the pandemic, providing feedback and allowing students to offer feedback required a different approach for many teachers. No longer could a student easily turn to a fellow in-person learner to complete a Think-Pair-Share activity. As teachers explored new ways to share and facilitate student-to-student discourse and feedback in a remote environment, the importance of clear protocols for engaging with feedback came to light. Learning protocols are nothing more than a series of steps or expectations used to structure learning conversations and learning experiences. Protocols ensure that learning is efficient, purposeful, and productive. Protocols also hold students responsible and accountable for their learning. Protocols model and demonstrate how students can lead inquiry and lead their learning.

In the following sections, we'll examine feedback protocols that were successful during the pandemic for blended, distance, and remote learning, as well as can be used during in-person learning:

- Prompts and Cues

- Tuning Protocol

- Sixty-Second Synchronous Interviews

- Dialogue Journals

- Gallery Critique

Feedback Protocol #1: Prompts and Cues

Fisher and Frey (2007) concluded that when students learn how to think about their mistakes and errors, it saves time and prevents students from developing "learned helplessness," a condition in which students depend on adults for the "right" information. Each one of us makes mistakes and does our best to catch them. Typically, mistakes are due to a lack of attention and a lack of focus. For example, you might forget to put the milk back into the refrigerator because you got distracted. If someone brings that error to your attention, you might feel a bit annoyed at first, think the person is an unhelpful nagger, and ask, "Are you sure I left the milk out? I always put it back." On the other hand, if you're open and ready to receive feedback, you'll immediately recognize the error and know what it takes to correct it.

Learners of all ages (adults and students) make mistakes because of fatigue, distraction, or inattention, and as a result, their performance suffers. However, learners often possess the knowledge and skills needed to avoid the mistake in the first place by merely paying more attention. You know that milk stays fresh by staying in the refrigerator, and you also know how to put the milk in the fridge; you might just need to be more present in the situation.

On the flip side, errors can occur because of a lack of knowledge or skill. Even when it's brought to your attention, sometimes you aren't quite sure what to do to fix a problem. If students lack the skills or conceptual understanding to do anything differently, when given another opportunity, they may become paralyzed. Imagine if you tell a student to bake a cake, and the cake doesn't rise. You then say, "It didn't rise; go back and do it again." The student could hypothesize that more sugar is needed for the cake to rise and test this hypothesis, only to discover that, again, the cake didn't rise.

In this instance, the feedback wasn't specific nor actionable; in fact, it was anything but feedback. As this example illustrates, correcting mistakes while failing to address errors can be a costly waste of valuable instructional time.

In this example, the error was caused by the student's lack of knowledge about the chemistry that's taking place. Giving feedback on baking powder and its impact on the baking process would be a great reteaching opportunity to address the student's understanding. This is also an opportunity to use inquiry-based questioning to help the student assess their thinking process. For instance, you might inquire, "Of the ingredients used, which ingredient or ingredients causes the cake to rise? Take a few minutes to research each of the ingredients used to bake a cake. Look at the chemical reactions of each ingredient, and see if you can determine which might help the cake to rise." Correcting errors results in new understanding and improved performance; moreover, once you implement this practice, students rarely make the same errors again.

Prompts are statements or questions that impel students to do cognitive or metacognitive work. Sometimes prompts draw on background knowledge ("Remember when we read, we circle words that we aren't sure about…"). When looking at a student's math solution, you might say, "I see there is only a number here in the answer." The student may immediately respond, "Oops, it's 25 centimeters; I forgot the units!" This would indicate that this was a mistake for this student, not an error. You might say about another student's problem, "I see an accurate answer, but I do not see any of your solution paths." The student might then respond, "I wasn't sure how to work this problem, so I just asked Shania for the answer." You could then work on the problem with the student and ascertain the learning gap.

Alternatively, cues are shifts in learners' attention. Cues are more direct than prompts and include a range of strategies such as verbal, gestural, physical, visual, and environmental cues. You can cue students to specific passages in the text, use inflections in your voice to emphasize particular parts, and use gestures to help learners notice ideas and information. For the math example, you could tap the paper next to the answer, signaling for the student to write down units.

Prompts and cues are more effective than merely correcting or pointing out a mistake. When prompts and cues are used effectively, they support students in using various approaches to arrive at a solution and generate claims to defend it. Students learn to value the teacher's perspective and their peers when analyzing problems, generating conclusions, and determining solutions. In this instance, students are conditioned to view learning as a process where mistakes happen and being "wrong" is part of that process.

Feedback Protocol #2: Tuning Protocol

The Tuning Protocol, a well-known discussion protocol developed by McDonald et al. (2003), offers a supportive structure that facilitates productive dialog and conversation. The Tuning Protocol helps structure group discussions by:

- Defining a sequence of discussion prompts

- Structuring time (allocating a set number of minutes for each section of the discussion)

- Defining roles (assigning particular perspectives or responsibilities to various students)

- Defining norms for listening and exchanging ideas

The following is an adapted and enhanced presentation of the protocol.

TUNING PROTOCOL

Adapted from McDonald, Mohr, Dichter, & McDonald, 2003

Introducing (four minutes)

The Tuning Protocol can organize meaningful feedback on any initiative, topic, concept, or project. First, the student-presenter offers an overview of their work, project, or idea and shares some thinking about fundamental design principles for the learning task. The student-presenter then frames a question to guide the conversation. During the pandemic, the following question might guide the Tuning Protocol for a COVID-19 health and safety public service announcement, "How can we encourage our communities to follow health measures such as wearing a mask and maintaining social distancing?" In an early phase of planning a project, meanwhile, a dilemma question from a student-presenter might be, "Where would the most useful critique points in this project be?" As the student-presenter shares the prompt, other students are entirely silent and actively listening.

Clarifying (two minutes)

Student-participants then ask clarifying questions of the student-presenter regarding the initiative, topic, concept, or project. For example, a student-presenter might inquire or ask, "What is a pandemic?" Clarifying questions from student-participants should be brief, short, and related to the introductory information shared by the student-presenter.

Probing (three minutes)

Student-participants ask probing questions of the student-presenter, such as:

- What scientific evidence will support your health and safety recommendations?
- How will you create an emotional response and call to action?
- What medium will you use to describe the benefits of COVID-19 precautions?
- Will the imagery in your public service announcement illicit a strong response to change behavior?

Probing questions help the student-presenter expand their thinking, offering feedback for improvement purposes. Be sure that student-participants avoid questions that are advice in disguise, such as, "Why don't you think about swapping that image for something more visceral?"

Discussing (ten minutes)

Student-participants discuss the work that has been presented and explore solutions to the student-presenter's topic or question. Student-participants direct comments to each other, not the student-presenter. During this time, the student-presenter physically distances from the group (for example, backing their chair away, turning around, or disabling the camera function in an online, synchronous session). The student-presenter remains silent and takes notes on the student-participants' comments. This encourages student-participants to speak openly and engage in authentic conversation. More, this forces the student-presenter to actively listen without responding and influencing the direction of the discussion. For student-participants, it is helpful to begin with what went well. For example, "I like..." or "I like the strong message that is communicated" or "I like the solutions offered because..."

Reflecting (three minutes)

Next, the student-presenter has an opportunity to respond to items from the student-participant discussion. Student-participants are silent during the reflection step. The student-presenter then summarizes what they heard from the conversation and describes what the next steps will be. An example could be something like, "What I heard was that you liked the authenticity of this project and the strong emotional message that is conveyed. You were also concerned about not having enough tribal voices in the video. I will work with the local tribe to get more interviews for my video project."

Debriefing (three minutes)

The group debriefs the process, reflecting on how successfully student-participants adhered to the discussion norms and the tuning protocol.

Feedback Protocol #3: Sixty-Second Synchronous Interviews

Sixty-second synchronous interviews are a quick way to assess student understanding and offer individualized feedback. This protocol is very effective in the blended and remote space because it can be conducted through synchronous video conferencing. Sixty-second video interviews can also occur in person while other students are engaged in stations, projects, or personalized learning.

The sixty-second interview is a conversation between you, the teacher, and the student. The "interview" is framed by inquiry-based questions that help you assess current levels of understanding. The interview can be concise and powerful if thoughtfully developed and planned. Here are some critical questions to consider before hosting your first interview:

- What knowledge, task, process, or strategy do you want students to know or be able to demonstrate?

- What predetermined interview questions will assess student knowledge, task, process, or strategy?

- How can you sequence interview questions, from simple to complex, to determine levels of understanding?

- How will students demonstrate their learning during this quick formative check (draw something, talk through something, or the like)?

- How will you collect data during and after the interview? Note: Because the interview is short, we suggest that you wait until after the interview to record notes, draw conclusions, and plan next steps.

Interviews can easily go longer than sixty seconds, so you might want to set a timer for two minutes. The point is that you get a pulse check on how students are doing. If you teach secondary learners, you might have hundreds of students, so it's vital to determine how many interviews you will conduct and plan for success. You will likely encounter students who have significant gaps in their understandings of a concept. It's essential to take note and to go back and plan for differentiation and reteaching in small, focused group sessions.

Feedback Protocol #4: Dialogue Journal

A dialogue journal is a writing protocol that provides opportunities for the teacher and the student to write back and forth with one another. The journal is ongoing and helps you build relationships with each student while modeling writing and observing students' progressing skills. You begin by writing a starting entry, such as the following "Teacher Prompt" (Figure 8.1). We created this example using Google Slides, but feel free to use any online collaborative slide deck or document that works best for your classroom.

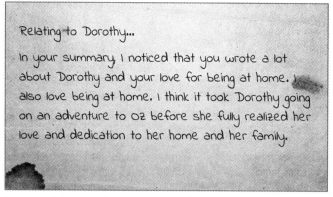

Figure 8.1. Teacher Prompt Example (Slide 1, Day 1)

Next, the student responds to the prompt with the following slide (Figure 8.2).

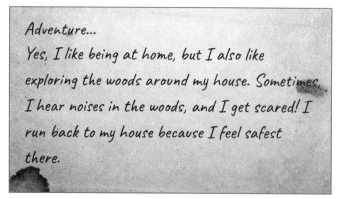

Figure 8.2. Student Response Example (Slide 2, Day 1)

The teacher and student will asynchronously add slides throughout the week. Take a moment to review both the prompt and response again—a dialogue journal in action. Dialogue journals are a great way to build positive and trusting relationships with students and to create a space for conversations about learning. As students become more comfortable sharing inside the dialogue journal, you can also incorporate more feedback into the entries, pushing student learning even further. Take a moment to consider the importance of establishing a safe and supportive culture for feedback. How might this protocol, if used early, begin building that desired state?

Feedback Protocol #5: Gallery Critique

In a gallery critique, students post work for others to review. In a blended learning classroom, the work can be published using Google Jamboard or Google Slides, for example, with each student having a dedicated jam or slide. A gallery critique works best when the goal is to identify and capture only positive features that can help all students improve, citing examples from only a small subset of the posted work. Viewing work from the entire class, you'll likely spot many opportunities for improvement, but this is not the time to try to point them all out.

A gallery critique aims to find useful ideas and strategies as well as examples of exemplars that students can borrow from to improve their work. If the work is visual, it can be posted for viewing in a gallery style. If the work is written, it can be posted on a wall or copied and distributed to students. For written work, short pieces or a portion of a larger piece, such as a multi-step word problem or a paper's thesis statement, work best and can be shared in a Google Docs document. The following table features an example gallery critique protocol.

GALLERY CRITIQUE

Adapted from Berger, Rugen, & Woodfin, 2014

Introduction (five minutes)
The teacher explains the protocols for a gallery critique and the learning outcome(s). The teacher reminds students of the protocols for giving feedback: Be kind, be specific, and be helpful.

Posting the Work (five minutes)
Each student copies and pastes their work on a slide.

Silent Gallery Walk (five minutes)

Students view all the drafts in a silent walk and take notes (for example, by using the sticky notes feature in Google Jamboard), identifying strong examples of a predetermined focus (descriptive language, use of evidence, elegant problem solving, experiment design, or the like).

What Did You Notice? (five minutes)

The teacher leads a discussion in person or using synchronous video technologies. Students cannot make judgments or give opinions; they can comment only on things they noticed and identified.

What Is Working? (Five minutes)

The teacher leads students in a discussion regarding which aspects of the posted drafts grabbed their attention or impressed them. Each time students choose an example, they need to articulate precisely what they found compelling, citing evidence and supporting details from the student work. If learners aren't sure, the teacher asks inquiry-based questions until students can point to evidence within the work of others. Teachers also point to examples they are impressed with and explain why. The teacher charts the insights to codify particular strategies that students can use to improve their drafts.

The gallery critique works well on written documents and on projects where students are justifying their solutions. The protocol is versatile and effective in an online or in-person environment. A blended learning adaptation would entail students posting their work and completing the Silent Gallery Walk asynchronously, and then your facilitating the remaining steps in person.

With the gallery critique, as with each of the protocols, one of the best ways to have consistent implementation in the classroom is for school leaders to model the feedback norms and protocols in collaborative meetings and professional development sessions. There must be a proactive and purposeful culture of continuous improvement with all teachers and staff members asking, "How is our feedback?" "How do we know if our feedback is successful?" and "How can we continually improve our feedback?"

Conclusion

This chapter has explored how to develop and sustain a thriving community and culture around teacher-to-student and student-to-student feedback. But what exactly does that community look and feel like relative to feedback? Consistent academic feedback illuminates the quality of student work and drives high expectations for student learning. With prompting, scaffolding, norm-setting, and reflection, students share constructive, actionable feedback with each other. When you embed feedback into classroom practice, students exhibit pride and ownership over their work and their learning. There is no question about evidence of learning in a thriving feedback community and culture. Nor do you have to wait for summative test assessment data to know and act upon student performance levels.

Communicating feedback with purposeful, affirming language is vital. Consider how words of affirmation from those you respect affect your perseverance and motivation; the same is true for students. The way people perceive their intelligence has a marked influence on their basis to learn now and in the future. As a teacher your words matter, so choose them wisely. We must all create feedback cultures that affirm and celebrate mistakes as an integral part of the learning process.

The goal is to foster and build an enduring growth mindset in students so that they believe they can learn and grow each and every day. Dweck (2007) concluded that praising students for their intellectual ability doesn't increase motivation and resilience but instead encourages a fixed mindset, a belief that the world is stagnant and doesn't or shouldn't change. In contrast, praising students for their effort and how they process learning (through reasoning, communication, perseverance, strategy, improvement, and so on) promotes sustainable motivation and a growth mindset. It communicates to students what they've done to succeed and what they need to do to achieve success again. So, as you continue reimagining instruction in your classroom, how will you grow and sustain a growth mindset in your feedback practices?

Reflecting for Professional Growth

- How do you define academic feedback?

- What are the essential components of academic feedback?

- How will you create optimal conditions for students to utilize feedback in your classroom?

- When should you differentiate feedback and how?

- How do you assess the quality of academic feedback that you are offering students?

CHAPTER 9

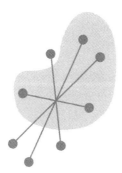

Integrating Digital Citizenship

Outcomes for Professional Learning

In this chapter, we'll discuss:

- Identifying digital age learning strategies and skills
- Building context for digital citizenship
- Framing digital citizenship
- Integrating digital citizenship into the classroom

CONNECTING TO THE ISTE STANDARDS FOR EDUCATORS

The content of this chapter relates to the following indicators:

Citizen (2.3.a) Educators create experiences for learners to make positive, socially responsible contributions and exhibit empathetic behavior online that build relationships and community.

Designer (2.5.c) Educators explore and apply instructional design principles to create innovative digital learning environments that engage and support learning.

Facilitator (2.6.a) Educators foster a culture where students take ownership of their learning goals and outcomes in both independent and group settings.

Facilitator (2.6.b) Educators manage the use of technology and student learning strategies in dig digital platforms, virtual environments, hands-on maker-spaces or in the field.

During the COVID-19 pandemic, we all worked with students and families who didn't yet have the skills needed to thrive in a remote or hybrid environment. Many districts quickly went 1:1, with some students and even families having, for the first time in their lives, access to learning technologies and the internet. The pandemic demonstrated that the digital divide wasn't a concept or theory; it was a reality for many Americans.

Teachers further discovered pockets of inequity in terms of student and family knowledge and skill about how to use and maximize blended and online learning tools. In response, educational leaders began deploying various types of supports for students and families experiencing challenges with their new learning realities. For instance, Metropolitan Nashville Public Schools launched Student and Family Support Centers across the city as well as online help options. Knowledgeable teachers and others staffed these centers daily, supporting students and families with basic technology skills and introducing digital age learning skills to many. The pandemic highlighted the need for universal student access to learning technologies and the internet as well as instruction in digital age learning skills.

In a broader sense, the pandemic demonstrated many opportunities to enhance digital citizenship. In reimagining our classrooms going forward, we must embed instructional practices that grow digital citizens, eliminate digital divides (both access and knowledge), and prepare students for living, working, and thriving in the future.

So, what's digital citizenship and why does it matter? Related to the Four Cs of the P21 Framework for 21st Century Learning—creativity, communication, critical thinking, and collaboration (Partnership for 21st Century Learning, 2019)—digital citizenship also factors in character and encompasses all aspects of appropriate technology use. It's directed toward students developing a strong commitment to digital ethics and etiquette in schools and society. Additionally, digital citizenship involves developing the research skills, fact-checking skills, and information analyst skills needed to learn and thrive in the digital age. It encompasses engagement in classroom discussions, a sense of belonging, and student aspirations and responsibilities.

Strategies and Skills for the Digital Age

Even before the pandemic, the world was speeding toward a new frontier, connecting and learning with technology in a variety of ways. Social media and digital storytelling now play an integral part in how students interact with the world. Creative expression and storytelling have become ubiquitous in society, and educators must foster creativity and self-directed learning to help students become idea creators and content developers. Exhibiting knowledge of these processes and strategies demonstrates the highest levels of understanding, so many of these practices deserve integration into the classroom.

Schools and districts are adopting a renewed focus on these digital age skills and digital citizenship because of the inequities brought to light during the pandemic. Educational leaders further recognize that the workplace of tomorrow is forever changed. Future success will depend on the ability to acquire new skills; complete project-based work; and inquire, think critically, and creatively solve problems. With today's global conditions, we educators need to consider how students interact with the world and begin thinking about change. Students are using powerful technology on a daily basis. They expect to have access to rich content in collaborative environments. They need to be prepared for their future, and the pandemic only demonstrated that we are failing many students in this regard. But don't lose hope just yet. For the first time in history, many districts and schools are equipped with the tools and supports necessary to make this critical course correction.

Digital citizenship is also a critical skill for tomorrow's leaders—and it's about more than online safety. Digital citizenship is about creating thoughtful, empathetic digital citizens who can wrestle with the important ethical questions at the intersection of technology and humanity. Early digital citizenship lessons and messages were focused on what not to do online—don't share personal information, don't post anything you wouldn't want your grandmother to read in the newspaper, etc. However, telling students only how not to use a tool doesn't help them learn to master it. So digital citizenship discussions need to focus on positive "do" statements. DigCitCommit, an initiative that provides resources on digital citizenship and digital competencies, supports this approach, shifting the conversation from don'ts to do's. Scan the QR code to learn more about this unique resource.

Building Context for Digital Citizenship

Rather than focusing on technology for technology's sake, embedding digital age skills into the curriculum should start with the learning outcomes the curriculum is meant to address. The success of implementing digital citizenship depends on thoughtful planning and wise decision-making about how to implement, to monitor, and to evaluate the effectiveness of learning. Key to using technology to its fullest potential are well-trained teachers supported by a school leader committed to change. The following list of guiding questions will help you identify how to integrate digital age skills, digital citizenship, and P21's Four Cs into your in-person, blended, or even remote learning environment.

BUILDING CONTEXT FOR DIGITAL CITIZENSHIP

- What are the realities of the current technology-immersed environment in which today's learners are growing up in? How should instruction be responsive to this reality?

- How can you leverage digital age skills and the Four Cs to scaffold and design learning experiences where students connect more deeply to content in more meaningful ways?

- How do teaching, learning, collaboration, and environment connect with one another?

- How can you provide students a more meaningful voice in their learning?

- How can you reimagine curriculum and instruction as a strategy for richer understandings?

- What should be assessed and what are the best ways to do so?

- How do you design experiences for how students learn today as well as what students need for future success?

Before you ask students to start producing, it's essential to build context for why they are creating in the first place. Students will be far more willing to engage in self-directed learning, displaying determination and grit, if they understand what problem is being solved and why their voice is needed to address it.

Framing Digital Citizenship

In a thriving community, every citizen contributes to the greater good of the community. We all celebrate each other's strengths, and help people find roles that suit their personality and interests. To create responsible citizenship, the classroom, too, must become a community. The biggest challenge teachers are facing right now—especially so during the pandemic—is active and responsible participation in learning. Classrooms should be learning communities, in which students rise to the challenge of exercising digital citizenship when allowed to choose and use the tools in their own learning journeys.

In a blended learning environment, where the digital and brick-and-mortar environments work in tandem, digital citizenship is really just citizenship. Active engagement in a blended learning classroom (as in any classroom and all academic and non-academic areas as well), is closely aligned to students' ability to make positive choices while understanding how their choices align with social norms. Students, as effective collaborators and digital citizens, recognize there are many ways to solve problems, interpret text, draw conclusions on data, reason through new scenarios, and understand that the methods of fellow students (citizens) can help them identify new ways of thinking and learning. Academic conversations wrapped in empathy and active listening are critical skills when collaborating with student peers, and those skills will carry well beyond the classroom and directly into college and career.

The following list of activities offers ideas for building digital citizenship and promoting responsible decision making, self-management, and relationship building in your classroom.

ACTIVATING DIGITAL CITIZENSHIP

Activate with Fictional Stories

Read fictional stories about characters who solved problems in clever ways. Or discuss how novices persevered through challenges and difficulties to make a significant discovery. Based on facts and inferences, how did these individuals feel while solving problems and why did they solve problems in a particular way? Also inquire as to how students feel when faced with similar challenges.

Activate with Student Interests

Ask students to identify their own personal hobbies, interests, strengths, and weaknesses in general. Then ask students to use visual representations to quantify these characteristics by creating a video or slide deck.

Activate with Praise and Affirmation

Provide praise and affirmation to students when they persevere through challenging problems. Give authentic feedback, such as:

- When you had difficulty solving the math problem, you tried another problem-solving strategy and were successful at finding a solution. Your perseverance resulted in success!

- When you were unclear of the directions, you asked a friend instead of disengaging. Asking for help instead of giving up will get you far in life!

Activate with Storytelling

Tell stories about famous actors, actresses, mathematicians, scientists, humanitarians, and so on who showed respect for each other within a specific area of expertise, such as Blaise Pascal and Pierre de Fermat. Use examples of communication between thinkers to show how to have friendly debates without feelings getting hurt or people feeling criticized. For example, create a theoretical friendly debate of the theory of gravity between Isaac Newton and Albert Einstein (with the help of a bit of time travel).

Activate with Real-World Learning

Routinely ask students about real-world issues or problems that matter to them. How might they create inventive solutions? Group discussions such as these shed light on differing world views, personalities, and backgrounds of students and how they have similar or different experiences and preferences. Students earn from each other about why other concepts and problem-solving approaches are interesting, needed, and valuable.

Activate with Project-Based Learning

Use project-based learning experiences that draw upon mindsets and skills. Part of collaboration is deciding as a group how students plan to work together. Essentially, students are creating norms. This discussion prompts students to answer questions about how they best work in a group and illuminates individual collaborative skills.

Activate with Reflection

Encourage students to reflect on how they plan to approach learning that day. Morning meetings or closing circles are excellent uses of time for reflection. Or, students might individually reflect in their journals. Also, ask students to talk about risks they took that were successful or failures that they want to improve on.

Integrating Digital Citizenship into the Classroom

Learning flourishes when teachers create a calm, yet engaging learning environment that promotes a good balance between structure and autonomy. A well-organized digital learning space sends students a powerful and positive message: This space is designed specifically for you, with your specific needs in mind, because you and your learning are important. So how do you get there for your students?

Focus on collaboration. One of P21's Four Cs, collaboration is not only a life skill but also a life necessity. It's a core part of every career field and every academic discipline. Thus, it should be at the core of the classroom. More than ever, learning should be part of a social context, as learners collectively rely on each other's best thinking to solve complex problems. No matter what subject or concept you teach, collaboration is a crucial component. When students engage in collaboration, they experience the following (both in person or at home):

- Higher ownership and investment in their learning

- Increased efficiency and productivity, which translates into channeling cognitive energies into creative processes

- An increase in individual and collective efficacy

- Greater autonomy over the time, place, path, or pace of learning

- The ability to collectively collaborate and work together, using digital technologies in a blended or completely remote context

- Opportunities to grow and hone digital age skills, such as teamwork and cooperative learning

Before focusing on the structural aspects of blended learning (platforms, tools, and processes) there must be clear goals and outcomes about how teachers want learning or behaviors to change as a result of the blended learning environment. Here are some ideas to help you create a blended learning environment that promotes warmth, comfort, and collaboration.

INTEGRATING DIGITAL CITIZENSHIP INTO THE CLASSROOM

Digital Playgrounds

Provide a platform or digital playground just for fun and discovery. This could be a video creation platform or an online LEGO builder. Reasoning and problem-solving skills can be reinforced through creative and unstructured play in these settings.

Multiple Presentation Options

Provide flexibility in how students work and make thinking visible: multiple options for presentation (video creation, slides, online presentation, asynchronous collaboration, and more) and multiple means of expression (written, narrative, spoken, video, and so on).

Video Creations

Provide multi-modal directions through video creation. All students benefit from having visual cues that support textual instructions.

Morning Meetings and Closing Circles

Establish a familiar greeting with students and consistently hold morning meetings (virtually or in person) and closing circles each learning day.

Transitions and Routines

Create a slide that helps students transition during synchronous online or in-person meetings. This creates a safe structure that helps students stay focused and engaged during fishbowls, Socratic seminars, group projects, independent time, and so on.

STOP. REFLECT. PLAN. ACT.

Quality Feedback Essentials

Professional Learning Task. In this section, you began identifying ways to integrate learning activities that activate digital citizenship in your classroom. Using the below chart, **stop**, **reflect**, **plan**, and **act** upon your learning.

3	Identify three ways to integrate digital citizenship into your classroom.	1. 2. 3.
2	Share how you plan to integrate two of these ideas into practice.	1. 2.
1	What's one original idea missing from the list?	1.

Conclusion

As you integrate digital citizenship into your classroom, focus on:

The Who. When you are asking students to complete a task, what does your communication sound like? "I need you to do…" "I expect you to do…" "Bring me…" Notice the teacher-centric language in these statements? When the narrative is teacher-centric, the focus is on what the teacher wants the student to do. Being a productive citizen is born out of a student's intrinsic desire to do something meaningful based on who they want to become. When students are challenged to do something meaningful, you tap into their motivational energy to push past obstacles. Digital tools provide a platform for boundless innovation and creativity. For instance, student blogging and podcasting allows learners to showcase their voice and blog about their learning experiences.

The Why. "What am I supposed to do?" The who will provide aspiration for students to pioneer on their own. Once they understand the why, students will articulate what they will do next. Think about a rock climber and their goal of getting to the top. There is a goal to be achieved, an upward climb, but the steps taken are up to the climber. Sometimes the climber must traverse horizontally before moving upward. As the teacher, you can provide support from below, but ultimately, the steps are up to the climber (student). Ultimately, in a student-led environment, the climb (the what) will be up to the students.

The How. Technology tools can provide a sturdy bridge between context and content. Content alone is just a conglomeration of knowledge and skills, ready to be unpacked, applied, and transformed. The context—the how, or the medium by which students interface and engage with the world—paired with content in transformational ways can pivot content from an amalgam of information to a collection of dynamic and meaningful learning experiences. When you focus on the how, you connect learning objectives to instructional strategies that ensure students are creating new solutions to problems that matter. Additionally, you are positioning skills to be mastered in the context of innovation and complex thinking—tools that learners will need to succeed in the future.

Reflecting for Professional Growth

- What does digital citizenship mean to you, and how does it transcend the traditional definitions?

- How does digital citizenship relate to the 4Cs and digital age skills?

- Which digital age, 4Cs, or citizenship skills did your students need support with during the pandemic? How will you use what you've learned to continue growing those skills and abilities?

- What is the connection between digital citizenship and student engagement?

- What are practical ways to integrate digital citizenship into your blended classroom?

Epilogue

Unless you know the road you've come from,
you cannot know where you are going.

—AFRICAN PROVERB

We created this book as a guidebook to support you on your journey of implementing blended learning successfully in your district, school, or classroom. The tools it offers, however, will be only as effective as your shared attitudes, values, beliefs, purpose, and practices toward learning and using technology to enhance learning for students. As you plan and implement strategies found in this book, we ask you to make three commitments.

Commitment 1: Commit to Yourself

You must ensure your own beliefs and habits of mind are explicitly identified and examined in order to shape the school's or classroom's culture around teaching and blended learning.

IDENTIFYING YOUR PURPOSE

To determine your purpose, answer these questions:

- Why did I choose to be an educator?
- What is it that I uniquely bring to the profession?
- Why must I use technology to enhance learning?
- What challenges am I willing to face because I have chosen to coach?
- How is teaching bigger than myself?

My purpose is:

As young teachers early in our careers, we were both faced with opportunities that resulted in reexamining our teaching practices. I (Nathan) vividly recall the moment I re-examined my teaching practice. A student walked into class and proclaimed, "This class is boring."

That hurt. In a knee-jerk fashion, I said, "Okay, what do you want to do today?"

The student answered, "I want to go outside."

"All right, let's go outside," I said, then started thinking quickly about how the day's lesson would work outside. It wouldn't. I had to throw out my plans, but... I had just recently become certified to test water quality and already had outdoor kits organized. I took my students to the nearby bayou, and they tested it for E. coli, phosphates, algae, and more. The students had a blast and could finally see connections to what they were doing in the chemistry lab. That day changed the course of teaching for me. Every day could be an opportunity to actively learn in meaningful and engaging ways. In that moment I remembered why I had become an educator: to make a difference.

Around the same time, I had a mentor teacher that served as an instructional coach. She helped me shift the culture of the classroom from one where I was always seen as the expert to one where students were learning to become experts and I was serving as an activator of learning. I started shifting my instruction where students worked collaboratively on problems, tasks, and lab experiments. Students shared and compared their strategies and processes, discussing which methods were most easily understood and which were most efficient. My mentor inspired and encouraged me as I facilitated instruction in a way that ensured all of my students experienced and learned meaningful science concepts. This is an example of how I had the opportunity to examine my assumptions, beliefs, and habits and began to shape my classroom culture to be a more student-centered classroom.

Commitment 2: Commit to Your Colleagues

None of us teaches in isolation. That is one of the biggest lessons learned during the pandemic. We must each ensure a culture of reflection, refinement, and action focused on continuous improvement to have a successful blended learning implementation. Each cycle of collaborative learning and inquiry should be followed by reflection about what was learned both as individuals and collectively. This can serve as a springboard to future learning together. You and your colleagues must know when things are working and when things are not. Therefore, together you must create a culture where sharing problems, concerns, and data is the norm. You must also create norms that are collectively agreed upon by all team members, norms that enable team members to collectively and critically examine meaningful data and use that learning to challenge one another's thinking and to work together toward the improvement of blended learning.

One of the best things about being an educator is collaborating alongside your colleagues to help plan authentic projects and to examine student work products, to reflect and refine your practice with the goal of increasing student learning. In the most authentic sense, teachers find this collaboration so useful that they find time to have rich conversations and discussions outside of the scheduled Professional Learning Community (PLC) times. Think right now about how you will connect with your colleagues in meaningful ways. Will you use communication tools, like the ones your students are using? Will you collaborate with teachers in authentic ways, in the same way you are asking your students to collaborate?

Commitment 3: Commit to Your Students

Keep your classroom—whether physical, remote, or blended—student-centered. Reflect that in your language by transforming traditional teacher-centric expectations into student-centric aspirations (the following table provides some examples). Support your students in understanding the why of the tasks they're working on. Share what works for you to stay on task. (Those technology tools you use in the blended learning classroom happen to be great project management tools that help students prioritize and organize their work and collaborate with peers.) Connect what they're learning and the tools they're using to their lives beyond the classroom and real-world problems to motivate them and show their learning matters.

When students are inspired to do something meaningful, you tapped into their motivational energy to push through challenges and obstacles, which provides a platform for boundless innovation and creativity.

STUDENT-CENTRIC ASPIRATIONAL STATEMENTS	
Instead of...	Say this...
"I expect you to pay attention."	"How does it make you feel when others are listening to you?"
"I expect you to do better."	"How are you using feedback to grow as a learner?"
"I like that you always are on time to class."	"You are showing personal responsibility through your punctuality."

Students will persevere through the challenges presented in remote, distance, or blended learning when they feel supported and when they understand the *why*. Think about a rock climber and their goal of getting to the top. There is a goal to be achieved, an upward climb, but the steps taken are up to the climber. Sometimes the climber must traverse horizontally before moving upward. A teacher can provide support from the ground level, but ultimately, the steps are up to the climber. Ultimately, the steps (the "what") will be up to the students in a student-centered environment. Check in with your students frequently to ask them why they are completing a task. If they are struggling to articulate this, then help remind them of the *why*.

Instructional and learning technology can provide a sturdy bridge between context and content. Content alone is just a conglomeration of knowledge and skills, ready to be unpacked, applied, and transformed. The context (the "how," or the medium by which students' interface and engage with the world) paired with content in trans-formational ways can pivot content from an amalgam of information to a collection of dynamic and meaningful learning experiences. When we focus on the "how," we connect learning objectives to instructional strategies that ensure students are creating new solutions to problems that matter. Additionally, we are positioning skills to be mastered in the context of innovation and complex thinking.

When promoting and cultivating student-led classrooms, it's important to remember that the teacher's role has never been so crucial. Thank you for taking this journey with us, for taking a risk through your focus on innovation to make learning more authentic for students. You are not only helping students achieve learning goals, you're helping them to build the skills that will help them be successful in work and in life.

References

Alliance for Excellence in Education. (n.d.) *A 5 step process for creating your future ready action plan.* Future Ready Schools. dashboard.futurereadyschools.org/5steps

Anderson, L. W., & Krathwohl, D. R. (Eds.). (2001). *A taxonomy for learning, teaching, and assessing: A revision of Bloom's Taxonomy of educational objectives.* Longman.

Bloom, B. (1956). *Taxonomy of educational objectives: The classification of educational goals.* Longmans, Green.

Berger, R., Rugen, L., & Woodfin, L. (2014). *Leaders of their own learning: Transforming schools through student-engaged assessment.* Jossey-Bass.

Borup, J., West, R. E., Graham, C. R., & Davies, R. S. (2014, January). The adolescent community of engagement framework: A lens for research on K–12 online learning. *Journal of Technology and Teacher Education, 22*(1), 107–129. editlib. org/p/112371

Chappuis, S., Stiggins, R. J., Arter, J. A., & Chappuis, J. (2004). *Assessment for learning: An action guide for school leaders.* Assessment Training Institute.

Clayton Christensen Institute. (2021). *Blended learning models.* Blended Learning Universe. blendedlearning.org/models

Collaborative for Academic, Social, and Emotional Learning [CASEL]. (2019). *SEL 3 signature practices playbook: A tool that supports systematic SEL.* schoolguide.casel. org/uploads/2018/12/CASEL_SEL-3-Signature-Practices-Playbook-V3.pdf

Danielson, C. (2011, January). Evaluations that help teachers learn. *Educational Leadership, 68*(4), 35–49. eric.ed.gov/?id=EJ913793

Danielson, C. (2007). *Enhancing professional practice: A framework for teaching.* ASCD.

Dinmore, S. (2019). Beyond lecture capture: Creating digital video content for online learning – a case study. *Journal of University Teaching and Learning Practice, 16* (1). files.eric.ed.gov/fulltext/EJ1213966.pdf

Dirksen, J. (2016). *Design for how people learn.* New Riders.

Digital Promise. (2021). digitalpromise.org

Dorn, E., Hancock, B., Sarakatsannis, J., & Viruleg, E. (2020, December). *COVID-19 and learning loss—disparities grow and learning needs help.* McKinsey & Company. mckinsey.com/industries/public-and-social-sector/our-insights/covid-19-and-learning-loss-disparities-grow-and-students-need-help

Dweck, C. S. (2007). *Mindset: The new psychology of success.* Ballantine Books.

Ferlazzo, L., & Sypnieski, K. H. (2018, March 29). Activating prior knowledge with English language learners. *Edutopia.* edutopia.org/article/activating-prior-knowledge-english-language-learners

Fisher, D., & Frey, N. (2007, September). Implementing a schoolwide literacy framework: Improving achievement in an urban elementary school. *The Reading Teacher, 61*(1), 32–43.

Gannon, K. (2018). How to create a syllabus. The Chronicle of Higher Education. chronicle.com/interactives/advice-syllabus

Hattie, J, & Yates, G. C. R. (2014). *Visible learning and the science of how we learn.* Routledge.

Hattie, J. (2009). *Visible learning: A synthesis of over 800 meta-analyses relating to achievement.* Routledge.

Hess, K. K., Carlock, D., Jones, B., & Walkup, J. R. (2009, June). *What exactly do "fewer, clearer, and higher standards" really look like in the classroom?* [Whitepaper]. CCSSO, Detroit, MI. 01fd4346-c1b0-45d9-899e-3654cb2c37d5.filesusr.com/ugd/5e86bd_2f72d4acd00a4494b0677adecafd119f.pdf

Kuhfeld, M., Tarasawa, B., Johnson, A. Ruzek, E. & Lewis, K. (2020, November). *Learning during COVID-19: Initial findings on students' reading and math achievement and growth.* NWEA. nwea.org/content/uploads/2020/11/Collaborative-brief-Learning-during-COVID-19.NOV2020.pdf

Lemov, D. (2015). *Teach Like a Champion 2.0: 62 techniques that put students on the path to college.* Jossey-Bass.

Marzano, R. J. (2017). *The art and science of teaching: A comprehensive framework for effective instruction.* Solution Tree.

McDonald, J. P., Mohr, N., Dichter, A., & McDonald, E. C. (2003). *The power of protocols: An educator's guide to better practice.* Teachers College Press.

Nottingham, J. & Nottingham, J. (2017). *Challenging Learning Through Feedback.* Corwin.

Nyquist. J. (2003). *The benefits of reconstruing feedback as a larger system of formative assessment: A meta-analysis.* Vanderbilt.

Palloff, R., & Pratt, K. (2009). *Assessing the online learner: Resources and strategies for faculty.* Jossey-Bass.

Partnership for 21st Century Learning [P21]. (2019). *P21 Framework for 21st century learning.* Battelle for Kids. static.battelleforkids.org/documents/p21/P21_Framework_Brief.pdf

Popham, W. J. (2008). *Transformative assessment.* ASCD.

Renaissance. (2021). *How kids are performing: Tracking the school-year impact of COVID-19 on reading and mathematics achievement.* renaissance.com/how-kids-are-performing

Thompson, B. (2007, January). The syllabus as a communication document: Constructing and presenting the syllabus. *Communication Education, 56*(1), 54–71.

Tomlinson, C. A. (1999). *The differentiated classroom: Responding to the needs of all learners.* ASCD.

Vai, M., & Sosulski, K. (2016). *Essentials of online course design: A standards-based guide (2nd ed.).* Routledge.

Webb, N. L. (1997). Criteria for alignment of expectations and assessments on mathematics and science education. Research monograph number 6: CCSSO.

Wellman, B., & Lipton, L. (2004). *Data-driven dialogue: A facilitator's guide to collaborative inquiry.* MiraVia, LLC.

Zubizarreta, J. (2004). *The learning portfolio: Reflective practice for improving student learning.* Anker Publishing Company.

Index

NUMBERS

1:1 program

implementing, 23

managing, 25

3-2-1 closure strategy, 118

5 Step Planning Process, 23–24

A

A La Carte, blended learning model, 21

academic competencies, including in pacing
    guides, 77–78

academic feedback, 180. *See also* feedback;
    self-assessment and automated feedback

academic integrity policy, including in pacing
    guide, 83–85

academic vocabulary, building, 100–106,
    131–133. *See also* vocabulary instruction

Achievable learning outcomes, 50

Acknowledging and Affirming, feedback essential,
    183

Actionable and Active feedback, 183

Analyst, ISTE Standards for Educators

    academic feedback, 180

    assessments, 154

    blended learning models, 18

    pandemic-related lessons, 2

    scope and sequence, 46

Analyzing category, Bloom's Taxonomy, 52

Anchoring strategy, activating prior knowledge,
    100, 130

application of knowledge, 33

Applying category, Bloom's Taxonomy, 53

Assessment Design Plan tool, 172–176

assessment FOR learning, 161

assessment plan, creating, 168–176

assessments. *See also* Bloom's Taxonomy;
    formative assessments; self-assessment
    and automated feedback; summative
    assessments

    aligning, 59–62

    creating products, 167–168

    designing, 163–168

    digital products, 164

    and feedback, 4–5

    goal of, 162

    ISTE Standards for Educators, 154

    learning portfolios, 158

    measuring learning, 156–157

    overview, 9, 154–155

    performance tasks, 158

    previewing, 147–151

    researching topics, 167–168

    rubrics, 165–167

    student-created products, 159

    titles in pacing guides, 75–76

    video creation, 164–165

asynchronous and synchronous learning, 3

attention residue, 4

B

Be the Teacher closure strategy, 116

beginning with end in mind, 47, 59

Berger, R., Rugen, L., and Woodfin, L., 185, 197

biography, including in pacing guide, 70

biology mitosis lesson, 36

Black students, studies done about, 10

blended instruction

    academic vocabulary, 100–106

    Collaborator, ISTE Standards for Educators,
      92

    Designer, ISTE Standards for Educators, 92

    designing and delivering, 92–93

    engaging instruction, 106–111

    Facilitator, ISTE Standards for Educators, 92

    feedback and reflection, 120–121

    learning outcomes, 97–98

    optimism, 93–97, 115–120

    prior knowledge, 99–100

    student discourse, 111–114

blended learning models. *See also* planning
    essentials

    Analyst, ISTE Standards for Educators, 18

course objectives, 49
Designer, ISTE Standards for Educators, 18
devices, 23–24
digital infrastructure, 25
Enriched Virtual, 21
Facilitator, ISTE Standards for Educators, 18
Flex, 20
Flipped Classroom, 20, 106–107
growing professionals, 39–42
Individual Rotation, 20
instructional practices, 32–33
A La Carte, 21
Lab Rotation, 19–20
learning environments, 31–34
LMS (learning management system), 29–30
PD (professional development), 26–28
personalized learning, 34–39
planning and implementation overview, 22–23
preparing learners, 28–29
project management, 25–26
selecting, 21–22
Station Rotation, 19
student integration, 29–30
tasks for student engagement, 30–31
Blended Learning Project Management Checklist, 25–26
Bloom's Taxonomy, 50–54, 60–61, 169–172. *See also* assessments; formative assessments; self-assessment and automated feedback; summative assessments
Bridging strategy, activating prior knowledge, 100, 130

C
CARES Act, PPS (Portland Public Schools), 14
Carousel Brainstorming, 160
case studies
    Champlain Valley Union High School, 37–38
    PPS (Portland Public Schools), 13–15
CASEL (Collaborative for Academic, Social, and Emotional Learning), 8, 94
Challenging Learning Through Feedback, 120, 181
Champlain Valley Union High School, 37–38
chunking information, 56–58

Citation Style, writing essential, 143
Citizen, ISTE Standards for Educators, 202
Clarifying, Tuning Protocol, 193
clarity and simplicity, 2–3
class meetings, associating with optimism, 95
Clayton Christensen Institute, blended learning models, 19–21, 106
Clear and Specific, feedback essential, 183
closing with optimism, 115–120
closure, creating, 147–151
Cloud-Based Word Wall, academic vocabulary, 103
Cloze Passages, academic vocabulary, 101
collaboration, 6, 207–208
Collaborator, ISTE Standards for Educators
    design and delivery, 92
    virtual instruction, 124
collective wisdom protocol, 40–41
Commercial closure strategy, 119
commitment
    to colleagues, 212–213
    to self, 211–212
    to students, 213–214
communication expectations, including in pacing guides, 79–80
competency-based learning progressions, 37
consistency, 4
content planning, 46
course description, including in pacing guide, 69
course meeting patterns, including in pacing guide, 71
course objectives
    design tips, 48
    formulating, 47–49
    including in pacing guide, 69
    and learning outcomes, 55–56
course timeframe, including in pacing guide, 83
course title, including in pacing guide, 69
course-participation guidelines, including in pacing guides, 76–77
COVID-19 mitigation measures, 9
Creating category, Bloom's Taxonomy, 51
creating versus remembering, 51
critical thinking, engagement with, 32
Cues, feedback essential, 183

D

Daily Dozen Sentence Stems closure strategy, 117
Danielson, Charlotte, 161
day-in-the-life scenarios, 32
deadlines, including in pacing guides, 76
Debriefing, Tuning Protocol, 194
design framework
    academic vocabulary, 100–106
    engaging instruction, 106–111
    feedback and reflection, 120–121
    learning outcomes, 97–98
    optimism, 93–97, 115–120
    prior knowledge, 99–100
    student discourse, 111–114
Designer, ISTE Standards for Educators
academic feedback, 180
    assessments, 154
    blended instruction, 92
    blended learning models, 18
    digital citizenship, 202
    learning expectations, 66
    pacing guide, 66
    scope and sequence, 46
devices, identifying and deploying, 23–24
Dialogue Journal, feedback protocol, 196–197
Differentiated, feedback essential, 183
differentiation, personalized learning, 38–39
DigCitCommit, 204
digital citizenship
    activating, 206–207
    closing circles, 208
    collaboration, 207–208
    context, 204–205
    fictional stories, 206
    framing, 205–207
    The How, 210
    integrating into classroom, 207–210
    ISTE Standards for Educators, 202
    morning meetings, 208
    overview, 202–203
    praise and affirmation, 206
    presentation options, 208
    project-based learning, 207
    real-world learning, 207
    reflection, 207
    storytelling, 206
    strategies and skills, 203–204
    student interests, 206
    transitions and routines, 209
    video creations, 208
    The Who, 209–210
    The Why, 210
digital environments, engaging students in, 31
Digital Flashcards, self-assessment strategy, 144
digital infrastructure, establishing, 25
digital learning portfolios, 157
digital playgrounds, 208
Digital Promise, 41
Dinmore, Stuart, 107
Dirksen, J., 148
Discussing, Tuning Protocol, 194
disruption of education, 10
DOK (Depth of Knowledge), 168–169
Dorn et al., 11
due dates, including in pacing guides, 76
Dweck, C. S., 199

E

Edcamps, 41–42
education, disruption of, 10
ELA Standard, video creation as assessment, 165
Emoji formative assessment strategy, 159
emojis and optimism, 94
Emoticons closure strategy, 116
engaging instruction. See also instruction in small groups; student engagement; writing essentials
    Categorizing, writing structure, 135
    Causing and Affecting, writing structure, 139
    Comparing and/or Contrasting, writing structure, 137–138
    delivering, 106–111
    Evaluating, writing structure, 138
    lesson writing structures, 134
    overview, 134
    Sequencing, writing structure, 136
    writing essentials, 139–143
Enriched Virtual, blended learning model, 21
Evaluating category, Bloom's Taxonomy, 52

exemplars, dissecting, 32
Exit Slip closure strategy, 120
Extended Abstract SOLO level, 189
Extended Thinking, Webb's DOK, 169. *See also* think-alouds and read-alouds
Extending strategy for closure, 148

F

Facilitator, ISTE Standards for Educators
   design and delivery, 92
   blended learning models, 18
   digital citizenship, 202
   pandemic-related lessons, 2
feedback. *See also* academic feedback; self-assessment and automated feedback
   and assessment, 4–5
   checking for, 33
   defining, 181–182
   differentiating, 188–190
   as formative assessment strategy, 187–188
   ISTE Standards for Educators, 180
   norms, 185–186
   overview, 180–181
   prompts and cues, 191–192
   protocols, 190–198
   quality essentials, 182–185
   and reflection, 120–121
   and self-assessment, 143–147
   student to student, 186
   teacher to student, 186
   tuning protocol, 193–194
Ferlazzo, Larry, 99
Ferlazzo, L., & Sypnieski, K. H., 99
Fill in the Blank, self-assessment strategy, 144
Fishbowl closure strategy, 118
Fisher, D., & Frey, N., 60, 191–192
Flex, blended learning model, 20
Flipped Classroom, blended learning model, 20, 106–107
formative assessments, 156–157, 159–163. *See also* assessments; Bloom's Taxonomy; self-assessment and automated feedback; summative assessments
   "empathy" gap, 187
   feedback as, 187–188
Four Box Synectics closure strategy, 119

Four Cs of P21 Framework for 21st Century Learning, 203
Frayer Model, academic vocabulary, 7, 105, 132–133

G

Gallery Critique, feedback protocol, 197–198
Gallery Walk formative assessment strategy, 160
Google Classroom, 103
Google Docs, 101–105
Google Drawings, 103–104
Google Meet, 103
Google Slides, 101, 103, 105
grades earned, including in pacing guides, 76
grading scale and practices, including in pacing guide, 85
Grammar, writing essential, 140
greetings and optimism, 94–95
group experiences, 33
GRPQ (Guided Reciprocal Peer Questioning), 161
Guided Reciprocal Peer Questioning Using Probing Questions, 159
Guiding strategy, activating prior knowledge, 100, 130
Gymea Technology High, 155–156

H

Hattie, John, 32, 187
Healy, Nicole (Nikki), 96–97
Here's What, data analysis protocol, 162
Hess et al., 172
Hispanic students, studies done about, 10
HOTS (Highest-Order Thinking Skills), 51, 60, 148, 187. *See also* LOTS (Lowest-Order Thinking Skills)
Hull Sypnieski, Katie, 99
HyFlex classroom, 5

I

I Care Why? closure strategy, 116
Illustrating strategy, activating prior knowledge, 100, 130
Individual Rotation, blended learning model, 20
information
   chunking, 56–58
   retaining, 99

instruction in small groups, 33. *See also* engaging instruction
instructional practices, enhancing, 32–33
instructional videos, creating, 107–111
Integrating strategy, activating prior knowledge, 100, 130
intellectual behavior, levels of, 50–51
interruption of learning, 9–11
Introducing, Tuning Protocol, 193
Introduction, gallery critique, 197
ISTE Standards for Educators
    academic feedback, 180
    Analyst, 2, 18, 46, 154, 180
    assessments, 154
    blended instruction, 92
    blended learning models, 18
    Collaborator, 92, 124
    Designer, 18, 46, 66, 92, 154, 202, 180
    digital citizenship, 202
    Facilitator, 2, 18, 92, 202
    feedback, 180
    Learner, 2, 66, 124, 180
    learning expectations, 66
    pacing guide, 66
    scope and sequence, 46
    virtual instruction, 124
ISTE Standards for Students, Creative Communicator (6a), 165
IT (information technology) team, creating, 25
It Fits Where? closure strategy, 118

J
Jeopardy closure strategy, 116

K
Key Words closure strategy, 117
KIP Graphic Organizers, academic vocabulary, 104
knowledge. *See also* prior knowledge
    application of, 33
    and evaluation, 50–51
K-U-D (Know, Understand, and Do) Chart, 37–38
Kuhfeld et al., 10
KWLs (Know, Want to Know, Learned), 7, 160

L
Lab Rotation, blended learning model, 19
Labeling a Graphic, self-assessment strategy, 144
Leader, ISTE Standards for Educators, virtual instruction, 124
Learner, ISTE Standards for Educators
    academic feedback, 180
    learning expectations, 66
    pacing guide, 66
    pandemic-related lessons, 2
    virtual instruction, 124
learners, preparing for success, 28–29. *See also* online students; students
learning. *See also* personalized learning
    asynchronous and synchronous, 3
    interruption, 9–11
    and learning environments, 31–34
    measuring with assessments, 156–157
    personalization, 11–13
learning expectations, overview, 66–68
learning experiences, occurrence of, 46
learning loss, 9
learning outcomes
    communicating, 97–98
    constructing, 54
    and course objectives, 55–56
    creating for student learning, 49
    evidence of, 38
    for lessons in pacing guides, 74
    and virtual instruction, 125–129
learning portfolios, 158
learning profiles, managing, 30
learning progressions, competency-based, 37
Lemov, D., 46, 57, 59
Leroy, Sophie, 4
lesson titles, including in pacing guide, 73–74
lessons
    closing with optimism, 115–120
    introducing for virtual instruction, 125–129
lessons and units, organizing and sequencing, 56–59
"live" learning. See synchronous and asynchronous learning

LMS (learning management system)
    differentiating instruction, 124
    integrating students in, 29–30
    parent involvement, 66
LOTS (Lowest-Order Thinking Skills), 53, 60, 187.
    See also HOTS (Highest-Order Thinking
    Skills)

M

Marzano, R. J., 56–57, 99
Matching Items, self-assessment strategy, 144
Math Assessment Design Plan, 173–174
McDonald et al., 193–194
McKinsey & Company study, 10–11
Measurable learning outcomes, 50
memory, capacity of, 56
Mentimeter, 103
metacognition, 32
mitosis lesson, 36
Multiple Choice, self-assessment strategy, 145
Multistructural SOLO level, 189

N

names and motions, associating with optimism,
    95
naming conventions, following for unit titles,
    71–72
Nashville Public Schools, 202
national districts, number of, 9
ninth-grade biology mitosis lesson, 36
non-examples, dissecting, 32
Nottingham, James and Jill, 120, 181–182, 188
Now What, data analysis protocol, 163
Numbered Heads Together closure strategy, 120
Number-Presentation, writing essential, 143
NWEA study, 10

O

Objective, feedback essential, 183
objectives. *See* course objectives
On Your Way Out closure strategy, 116
online students, feelings of, 5. *See also* learners;
    students
"opportunity learning," 3

optimism
    closing with, 115–120
    opening with, 93–97

P

P21 Framework for 21st Century Learning, Four
    Cs, 203
pacing guide design essentials
    academic competencies, 77–78
    academic integrity policy, 83–85
    assessment titles, 75–76
    biography, 70
    checklist, 86–87
    communication expectations, 79–80
    course description, 69
    course meeting patterns, 71
    course objectives, 69
    course participation, 76–77
    course timeframe, 83
    course title, 69
    deadlines, 76
    Designer, ISTE Standards for Educators, 66
    discussion board expectations, 80–82
    due dates, 76
    grades earned, 76
    grading scale and practices, 85
    Leader, ISTE Standards for Educators, 66
    Learner, ISTE Standards for Educators, 66
    learning outcomes for lessons, 74
    lesson titles, 73–74
    overview, 66–68
    teacher contacts, 69–70
    teacher headshot, 70–71
    teacher name, 69–70
    technical requirements, 82–83
    template evaluation, 88–90
    unit descriptions, 72–73
    unit objectives, 73
    unit titles, 71–72
Palloff, R., & Pratt, K., 143
pandemic-related lessons
    assessment, 9
    asynchronous and synchronous learning, 3
    challenges and strategies, 5–6
    clarity and simplicity, 2–3

collaboration, 6
feedback, 4–5
ISTE Standards for Educators, 2
professional development, 4
read-alouds, 7
reflecting on, 12
reflection task, 12
SEL (social-emotional learning), 8
student products, 6
think-alouds, 7
well-being, 5
Paragraph Form, writing essential, 141
Parallel Form, writing essential, 142
Partnership for 21st Century Learning, 203
PD (professional development)
developing foundation for, 26–28
overview, 4
recommendations, 39–40
peer questioning using probing questions, 159
performance levels, 51
performance tasks, 157–158
personalized learning, 11–14, 33–39. *See also*
learning
Pineapple Chart, 40–41
planning essentials, 18–19. *See also* blended
learning models
playlists, 35–36
PLCs (professional learning communities), 40
PLNs (professional learning networks), 41–42
portfolios. *See* learning portfolios
Postcard closure strategy, 118
Posting the Work, gallery critique, 197
PPS (Portland Public Schools), 13–14
Prestructural SOLO level, 189
Pre-Teaching strategy, activating prior knowledge,
100, 130
prior knowledge, activating, 99–100, 129–130.
See also knowledge
Probing, Tuning Protocol, 194
problem-solving, engagement with, 32
Professional Development Program
Implementation Checklist, 26–27
professional growth
academic feedback, 200
assessments, 177
blended instruction, 122

design and delivery, 122
digital citizenship, 210
feedback, 200
lessons learned, 15
pacing guide, 90
pandemic-related lessons, 15
planning essentials, 43
reflecting for, 63
scope and sequence, 63
virtual instruction, 152
project management, 25–26
prompts and cues, feedback protocol, 191–192
purpose, identifying, 211–212

Q

QR codes
5 Step Planning Process, 23
Assessment Design Plan tool, 172
Blended Learning Project Management
Checklist, 25
Bloom's Taxonomy, 51–54, 169
CASEL's welcoming activities, 94
Course Objectives and Learning Outcomes, 55
Course Pacing Guide Template, 88
DigCitCommit, 204
Introducing Lessons and Communicating
Learning Outcomes, 126–127
Professional Development Program
Implementation Checklist, 26
Scope and Sequence Template, 58
SMART Learning Outcome method, 50
Strategies for Opening with Optimism, 94
Virtual Lesson Academic Vocabulary, 131
Virtual Lesson Assessment Preview Section,
149
Virtual Lesson Introduction Section Template,
128
questioning strategies for self-assessment,
144–145
Quick Doodles Doodle closure strategy, 118

R

read-alouds and think-alouds, 7
reading scores, studies done about, 10
Recall and Reproduction, Webb's DOK, 169

Reflecting
strategy for closure, 148
Tuning Protocol, 194
reflection
and digital citizenship, 207
and feedback, 120–121
reinforcing
feedback, 183
strategy for closure, 148
Related learning outcomes, 50
Relational SOLO level, 189
Remembering category, Bloom's Taxonomy, 53
remembering versus creating, 51
Renaissance study, 10
research-based instructional strategies, 7
researcher findings, recommendations, 11
RSQC2 (Recall, Summarize, Question, Comment, Connect), 160–162
rubrics, developing for assessments, 165–167

S

San Gabriel Unified, 2–3
scenarios, day in the life, 32
Science Assessment Design Plan, 175
scope and sequence
aligning assessments, 59–62
Analyst, ISTE Standards for Educators, 46
course objectives, 47–49
Designer, Standards for Educators, 46
outcomes for student learning, 49–56
template, 58
units and lessons, 56–59
SEL (social-emotional learning), 3, 8
self-assessment and automated feedback, 143–147. See also academic feedback; assessments; Bloom's Taxonomy; feedback
self-care, prioritizing, 5
Sell It closure strategy, 117
Sentence Form, writing essential, 140
Silent Gallery Walk, gallery critique, 198
simplicity and clarity, 2–3
Sixty-Second Synchronous Interviews, feedback protocol, 195
Skills and Concepts, Webb's DOK, 169
small-group instruction, 33
SMART Learning Outcome method, 50, 97–98

So What, data analysis protocol, 162
SOLO (Structure of Observed Learning Outcomes), 188–190
Sorting, self-assessment strategy, 145
Specific learning outcomes, 50
Station Rotation, blended learning model, 19
Stiggins and Chappuis, 161
storytelling and digital citizenship, 206
Strategic Thinking, Webb's DOK, 169. See also think-alouds and read-alouds
student discourse, facilitating, 111–114
student engagement. See also engaging instruction
assigning tasks for, 30–31
continuing, 34
student learning, creating outcomes for, 49–56
student-created products, 6, 157, 159, 167–168
students. See also learners; online students
aspirational statements, 214
committing to, 213–214
integrating with learning environment, 29–30
LMS (learning management system), 29–30
"opportunity learning," 3
studies done about, 10
studies about learning disruption, 10–11
summative assessments, 156–158
Supportive, feedback essential, 183
Survival Words, academic vocabulary, 102
syllabus, articulating purpose of, 72
synchronous and asynchronous learning, 3, 107
synchronous interviews, feedback protocol, 195

T

tasks, assigning for student engagement, 30–31
teacher headshot, including in pacing guide, 70–71
teacher name and contacts, including in pacing guide, 69–70
technical requirements and support, including in pacing guide, 82–83
think-alouds and read-alouds, 7, 32. See also Extended Thinking; Strategic Thinking
Think-Pair-Share
closure strategy, 120
formative assessment strategy, 160
Thompson, B., 67, 90

Three Ws closure strategy, 118
Thumbs Up/Thumbs Down closure strategy, 116
Timely, feedback essential, 183
Timely learning outcomes, 50
Transition Integration, writing essential, 142
Tuggerah Public School, 111
Tuning Protocol, feedback, 193–194

U

unconferences, 41–42
understanding, checking for, 33
Understanding category, Bloom's Taxonomy, 53
Unexpecting strategy for closure, 149
Unistructural SOLO level, 189
unit descriptions, including in pacing guide,
    72–73
unit objectives, including in pacing guide, 73
unit titles, including in pacing guide, 71–72
units and lessons, organizing and sequencing,
    56–59
Unresolving strategy for closure, 149

V

Vai, M., and Sosulski, K.
    course objectives, 47, 49
    learning outcomes, 50
    pacing guides, 67
    units and lessons, 56–57
Vermont, competency-based education, 37
Video Creator tool, 101
Virtual Exit Tickets formative assessment
    strategy, 159
virtual instruction
    academic vocabulary, 131–133
    closure, 147–151
    engaging instruction, 134–143
    feedback, 143–147
    ISTE Standards for Educators, 124
    learning outcomes, 125–129
    lesson introduction, 125–129
    overview, 124–125
    previewing assessment, 147–151
    prior knowledge, 129–130
    self-assessment, 143–147
vocabulary instruction, 100–106. *See also*
    academic vocabulary

W

Webb, Norman, 168–169, 172
welcoming routines and optimism, 96–97
well-being, considering, 5
Wellman, B. & Lipton, L., 162
What Did You Notice? gallery critique, 198
What Is Working? gallery critique, 198
What Were You Doing? formative assessment
    strategy, 160
Whip Around closure strategy, 117
white students, studies done about, 10
wisdom protocol, 40–41
Word Cloud, academic vocabulary, 103
Wordle, 103
World Cafe formative assessment strategy, 160
writing essentials, 139–143. *See also* engaging
    instruction; student engagement

Y

Yates, Gregory, 187

Z

Zubizarreta, J., 158